MANGAL II

MANGAL II

Stories and Recipes

Ferhat Dirik and Sertaç Dirik

Photography by Justin De Souza

Foreword

Dalston to me is like Queens: rough, tough, and filled with thick pockets of anything you want in life. Stoke Newington Road reminds me of Jamaica Avenue with its yarn stores, all types of ethnicities selling their food within small spaces, lots of noise. And right there, in front of a bus stop, is where I found Mangal II.

Sertaç and Ferhat came into my life in my search for spinning meat and kebabs. I don't know if I stumbled into it, but I know, just like when Ed Lover and Dr. Dré shot the barbershop scene for 'Who's the Man?' and struck oil, I, too, hit the jackpot.

To see the meat being scorched over the coals, the tomatoes roasting, the different chops, the assembling of the doner, it spoke directly to my heart. They made us several huge platters of flesh – lamb chops, doner, chicken thighs, wings – with rice, tomatoes and peppers.

I am made of peppers, and I don't I think I have ever tasted spun meat that good. They pour their heart and soul into it – they are masters.

— Action Bronson

In Conversation with Ali: Part I

It has always been the dream of my father, Ali Dirik, to split his time between Turkey and England. After half a century of hard work, he is finally in a position where he can retire and indulge in a slower pace of life filled with hobbies like gardening and fishing. By 2023, for the first time in my thirty-five years of existence, he turned his dream to reality as he embarked to his beach house by the Aegean Sea for the best part of five months. My intention to interview him face-to-face was finally conducted in November of that year, upon his eventual return to London.

In a city full of Mangal-named restaurants, kebab houses, Turkish eateries and men named 'Ali', I've always wanted to promote my father's story. It is tragic, inspirational and, perhaps, common to the Anatolian diaspora. But through the lens of a Londoner, I always felt a sense of awe and bewilderment at how a person – with no formal education, who was working class and through sheer grit, talent and doggedness – managed to build the foundations for our restaurant and for my and siblings' lives. And, to the best of my ability, I recorded our conversation, transcribed it and translated pages of notes.

He's complex, remarkable and impossible to summarise in just a few pages, resulting in the omission of other notable details in his life in order to focus on his journey to Mangal II. There's no mention of his childhood shepherding alone in the mountains. Or any forensic dissection of his time in the army, where he became a senior line cook at the age of seventeen. We don't indulge in his impoverished upbringing in Turkey, nor do we particularly highlight his struggles of acclimatising to Britain. We've overlooked his hard drinking and smoking. And equally neglected to champion the extent to which he fed dozens (yes, dozens) of homeless individuals in Hackney for over twenty years. I don't believe these exclusions lessen him in any way. As the carnivorous man himself would prefer, we've stuck to the meat and none of the bones.

Let's tuck in.

Ferhat: OK, welcome Dad. I hope you might tell us about your early years in life.

Ali: From the moment I stepped on this Earth? Ah, OK, the early beginnings. I was born in 1963 in Sarız, a town just outside of the city of Kayseri and a place with tough, hard winters. We were a large family, and I had many siblings. Due to the difficult conditions in Sarız, my father relocated us to another district where the government provided housing for our family. So we settled in Pınarbaşı. When we were young, we would help my father with his workload so we, too, could provide for the family. I was a shoe-shine boy, a water-bottle seller, an intern at Dad's butchery.

F: This actually leads me to my next question. What made you enter the restaurant industry?

A: Years later, I found a restaurant job as a kitchen porter because Dad had a temper. There were very few types of jobs available where we lived. You had a choice: you either worked in a coffee house or a restaurant. And it wasn't even a proper restaurant with a full menu but a *lokanta*, a worker's canteen where they'd serve stews and casseroles. I was in an entry-level position, working both as a kitchen porter and assistant. We weren't just washing dishes; we'd also be learning basic food prep like peeling onions, potatoes, vegetables, everything. We had to organise all the soup ingredients, too. This was to prepare us to eventually become chefs one day. Soon, I was learning how to make stews and types of meats and cuts. And, for this reason, I feel very fortunate to have started in a lokanta. I eventually became a partner – on a very small scale – and even had my own apartment. It was small and always busy. It lasted nearly two years, until I left for the military.

F: You did your military service, but did you return after your service?

A: No. I felt the limitations. I couldn't cook many things; I couldn't source many ingredients. My professional ambitions outgrew what was on offer. I wanted more freedom: a better life, a better wage, greater opportunities to advance my skills. I decided I would move to Istanbul after my time in the military.

F: It seemed you wanted to further yourself. Did you go to Istanbul directly after your service?

A: I moved straight away after I was discharged.

F: How old were you at the time?

A: When I moved to Istanbul, I was around twenty-one. And as soon as I arrived, I went door-to-door asking for a restaurant job. With a stroke of luck, I was offered a job as an assistant chef at a trendy Istanbul restaurant. It was called Hacı Bozan Oğulları and patronised by rich people of Turkish society. It was there I discovered the many types of Turkish kebabs.

F: Was it an ocakbaşı style?

A: No. The gas grills were against the wall, and they had a brigade of thirty chefs!

F: That's a big team.

A: It was! I worked as an assistant chef for six months before I was paid a regular chef's salary.

F: Wait. So, you were like a lowly paid intern for the first six months?

A: Yes, sure... but I was open to learning and developing my technique. I reached a real chef's level. My foundation was in stew cooking and kebabs – I already knew these well. After working in this Istanbul restaurant, I made a move to a restaurant below a hotel. It was called Baran Ocakbaşı.

F: Did you join there in a higher position?

A: Yes. I was the one responsible for the kitchen, like a head chef.

F: And was this the first time you had your own team and menu? Or did the owners decide on these things?

A: The owners never chose the menu. They lived abroad in Europe and didn't work in hospitality. We created the menu.

F: And how old were you by this time?
A: I was twenty-three. I had met my wife, your mother, in Istanbul, and we had just gotten married. Your sister, Ayşegül, was born there.

F: Then you ended up in London? Weren't you head-hunted by someone who was impressed by your skills and prepared to move you here?
A: A week after Ayşegül's first birthday, I moved to London and left my wife and daughter behind. With the help of two colleagues and an intermediary, I received all the paperwork for a special work visa to immigrate to the UK. The intermediary, a businessman, met me in Istanbul and brought me to London. He covered all the costs, too.

F: How did you find the UK?
A: Difficult. I moved to the UK under very tough circumstances. I did not speak the language. I was alone. The climate, culture and lifestyle were so different. Yes, I knew a few people, but it wasn't enough. I had to start all over again.

F: Perhaps your mind was stuck in Istanbul. You had your wife, your baby daughter.
A: My mind was always with my wife and daughter.

F: Where were you first working in London?
A: I started working at 01 Adana in Newington Green, where my friend also worked. It was a classic kebab joint. Three years later, I opened my first restaurant, Mangal Ocakbaşı, with a partner.

F: I'd like to know more about that. You were new to the country with a limited network, no backer or any security. Mum and Ayşegül had, by this point, joined you in London.

Where did you find the confidence to open a restaurant, considering the factors at play back then?
A: In those first few years I was in London, I noticed it lacked a barbecue style like ocakbaşı. I had saved some money and trusted my experience. I was quite confident we could achieve something good. I took the step.

F: You went in with a partner?
A: He was a colleague from work, a friend who I trained. I chose him to be involved.

F: You must have got on well.
A: We did. He was always respectful towards me. We took that first step together by opening Britain's first ocakbasi (and Mangal) ever... in Dalston. It had just three tables and sixteen covers. We took over the lease, and I drew up the project and the kitchen plan. We opened the UK's first ever ocakbaşı.

F: The UK had never had an ocakbaşı before. This was a huge risk, and you had no back-up plan. I really am curious – did you have any fears?
A: No. I had no fears. I relied entirely on my skills, my profession. If it failed as a business, I could work as a chef somewhere else. At that time, there were very few chefs in London, in England, who could work to my standard. There was a high demand for chefs back then, so I could find work if this failed.

F: And you opened. Mangal was an immediate success. Did the degree or level of it surprise you?
A: I believed it would work.

F: And did you expect the British public to receive it so well?
A: England didn't have anything like it. First of all, our Turkish community supported this cooking style because the flavours were familiar. The restaurant received a lot of attention from the day it opened. This unknown cooking style, with wood converted into charcoal fire, was unique.

We introduced thirty-five types of kebabs, using special meats such as Scottish and Irish lamb. The customers loved it! Our customers were promoting our restaurant more than we were! That's how we started.

F: So you kept this going for five years?
A: I worked at Mangal, maintained a team and trained multiple chefs in this style for five years. I trained all the staff. They assisted but I still did all the prep, cooking and grilling. On average, I was working sixteen hours a day, maybe more. But it was worth it. I received praise from the public and attention from national and international media. We had a lot of attention, and we were rewarded with many loyal customers.

F: After, of course quite a bit of time passed, you opened your next restaurant.
A: I opened Mangal I in 1989, the year you were born. And I opened Mangal II, five years later, soon after Sertaç was born.

F: Now, what was the idea, the concept, the philosophy behind Mangal II that distinguished it from Mangal I. And what prompted you to open a second restaurant.
A: Well, the seating capacity at Mangal I was too small.

F: And, to clarify, you opened Mangal II with the same business partner?
A: Yes, the same person. I wanted a larger second branch. Three years later, we decided to split the partnership.

F: To essentially divide the restaurants?
A: That's right. I left Mangal I to my partner, and I took ownership of Mangal II.

F: How did you feel about giving up Mangal I?
A: It was my first love, but I felt restricted there. I wanted to expand and have a more spacious setting for my customers. I wanted a larger kitchen and menu that would showcase more dishes to the customers.

F: Was the plan for Mangal II always in the back of your mind? The underlying principle behind Mangal II was all about creating a menu with greater depth.
A: Yes, what we could sell at Mangal I was limited. Mangal II had more variety and launched with an expanded menu.

F: It seems you wanted to be more expressive as a chef by offering more dishes. How did you expand the menu? With more mezzes, salads, veggie options and doner kebab?
A: Yes! I wanted a grander menu. Mangal II gave me the space.

F: And when you first opened, how was the reaction?
A: Very good. I could express my intentions to my customers with a larger menu and dining area.

F: The setting at Mangal II was slightly more formal, from tablecloths to nuanced lighting. Did this restaurant reflect your ambitions, principles and standing in life?
A: Yes. It was like the settings of the restaurants I had worked at in Istanbul. I was accustomed to working in more refined environments.

F: It sounds like Mangal II was your end goal but Mangal I happened to be the stepping stone to achieving it.
A: Absolutely. Mangal I was the beginning. But the actual dream, where I could implement my desires, was Mangal II.

Opposite page
From top, clockwise:
Mangal II launch, 1994; Ali *(left)* and manager Emir *(right)* at the restaurant, 1994; Ali on the grill, 1994; Ali at the restaurant, 2012; Mangal II launch.

F: Knowing this must've made it easier for you to divide up the restaurants. You knew the type of establishment you wanted to form and the menu you wanted to cook. It was found in Mangal II, which must've given you peace of mind.

A: Yes, my son. Exactly that.

F: Soon thereafter, Mangal II is established. You're working hard and the restaurant is gaining popularity, especially amongst intellectuals, art dwellers and foodies. Plus, you're raising a family. How did you manage to balance it all?

A: It was hard. Back then, when I was young and energetic, I was ambitious in my profession. I worked hard and had to care for my family, restaurant and staff, who happened to be the most challenging. I constantly had to train them, keep difficult staff members under control and make them happy. These were very difficult conditions.

F: But you always loved your job, your industry, your service. Was it worth it?

A: I loved my career. Everyone should work in a job that they love. If you don't love what you do, you can never succeed at it. One must also serve the dishes one loves. These are my principles. I stuck to them.

F: You continued with the restaurant for many years. As time passed, I started coming to the restaurant and then Sertaç followed suit when he was older. What was that like for you?

A: It was a great source of happiness and strength. My sons were excited about my career: they came in and helped to build that base. It filled me with hope and joy that my career and efforts would not go to waste. You started here when you were eleven. Then Sertaç followed years later. I was proud to have my sons work with me because it was what I knew. I had done the same as an apprentice at my father's butchery. The experience of having my sons involved provided me with better morale. I could also spend more time with them. It made me happy.

F: Eventually, we grew up. I worked at the restaurant after uni. Sertaç was an adolescent. Then I became a dad. These years passed. By this time, were you mentally inching your way towards retirement? Had you been planning it for a while?

A: I always had a plan in the back of my mind. When you enter life's hardships and responsibilities, exhaustion eventually takes hold. I felt a desire to rest and to pursue other interests such as travelling, fishing and gardening. My sons chose to follow my path and I am grateful that their own dreams have given me this opportunity.

F: Well, we would never have had the chance to provide that for you without your endeavours. We are so grateful to you as well.

A: It's important to mention that one of the luckiest moments of my life was to meet your mother. She made sacrifices, parented with so much effort and maintained our home. And if there was any profit, even if it was three cents, she looked after our finances and invested our savings wisely. I have such a dedicated wife. I am eternally grateful to her. I love her.

F: You eventually came to the restaurant less and less. You handed me more responsibility and relinquished some of the control. Sertaç moved to Copenhagen to develop his craft. What were your thoughts of this time?

A: Sertaç was after new opportunities, and I always knew he'd be successful. He was a high-achieving child and did well in all his interests: as a musician, a graphic designer, an artist. When he told me he was moving to Copenhagen to develop his skills and work in renowned restaurants, I encouraged him and supported his goals. When he felt ready to return to London, I knew he would honour our efforts with Mangal II and work with you, his brother. You were so successful in running a business and managing a team, but I was relieved that Sertaç acquired his skills as a chef. I felt comfortable handing over a thirty-year-old restaurant to you both. Watching all your success has made me a proud father.

F: Let's talk about the pandemic. At the beginning, when Sertaç returned to London, the business was obviously closed but we still went to work every day. He and I began discussing our dreams and ambitions for the restaurant and set out a plan to implement them. We reopened four months later with a new menu and a concept. How did you react to the initial change?

A: The restaurant was set in its ways for nearly thirty years. I expected things would eventually change because something new would come along. To be honest, I had a few fears at first. Our customers had a palate for the existing menu and flavours. But you were sensible about the change. Not everything happened at once. It was a slow evolution and transition from the old system to the new system. New customers, who were seeking something more modern, responded well to this change. They liked all the improvements, concept and cuisine. It brought me great relief.

F: When all came to fruition, it was hugely successful. Could you have imagined it ever blowing up the way it did?

A: You both were so decisive and confident with the family business, even during the pandemic. You made sacrifices and put in so much effort to keep the restaurant alive. You introduced many wonderful things to the public. You created things I could never have imagined. When I saw your determination and achievements, I was not at all surprised. You're confident, passionate and creative.

F: When you look at the restaurant's current iteration – the team, the menu, the customers – what comes to mind? What are your final thoughts?

A: I'm now certain that the both of you will have further success and that you're on the right path. I have no doubts. You were raised in the industry. You're both young, dynamic and experienced. Primarily, you have a passion for the industry, great creative skills and good intentions. I firmly believe in your continued success.

Page 18
From top, clockwise:
Mangal II launch, 1994; Savaş Ay at Mangal II, 1995; İbrahim Tatlıses (Turkey's most famous folk musician/artist), Ali (to his left), Rahim Cüce (to his right), et al, 1995; İbrahim Tatlıses with Ali, 1995; Savaş Ay interviewing İbrahim Tatlıses, 1995.

Page 19
From top, clockwise:
Ali Dirik on the grill, 1998; Ali with Ferhat, 1995; Ali, 1998; Family meal with Cemile Dirik, Aunt Ayşe Kartal, our sister Ayşegül Dirik, Ferhat, Sertaç and Ali Dirik, 2000; Ali (centre) with his brother Hasan Hüseyin (left) and their uncle Haydar (right), 1995.

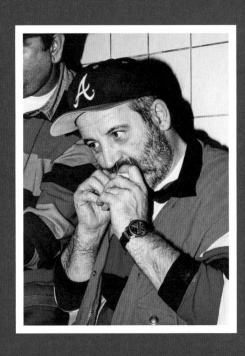

FOUNDATION
Old School

Mangal II was founded by our father in 1994 on Stoke Newington Road in the heart of Dalston. The word *mangal* refers to the type of grill we use in Turkish cooking, about 1–3 metres/3–10 feet wide, whereby *maşa* (cast-iron or stainless-steel grill tongs) are used to push charcoal around to adjust the temperature. Our open-fire grill restaurant, called *ocakbaşı* in Turkish, was the first of its kind in the UK; our dad, Ali Dirik, understood the potential and importance of this cooking style, which is countrywide today. The process of cooking everything with skewers over white-hot lumpwood charcoal means that the meat rarely rests on the metal and only cooks on the residual heat of the lit charcoal – a very pure way of tasting the food served.

The restaurant had white tablecloths, the waiters wore smart shirts and it was renowned for cooking some of the best Turkish food in London. For twenty-six years, it operated as a classic ocakbaşı; the menu was barely adjusted or tampered with. You could sit by the mangal and watch the show: the chef banging the skewers on the grill to remove the excess rendered fat and moving them from right to left as the conveyor belt of heat finishes off the multiple orders for grilled meats. It's like watching a five-hour drum solo.

The finale, to be served: tender grilled lamb and chicken straight from the mangal alongside an assortment of hot and cold mezze – all served with Turkish *pide*, the bread that has been resting on the grilled meats, absorbing the juices and catching smoke from the drips of fat hitting the coals. Perfection.

— Sertaç

Recipes

Ode to Dalston

Walk. Stumble up and down the high street and be on edge as you pass Dalston Kingsland station, where you're exposed to a box of crazy. Visit the wonders of London Fields to see the stream of young creatives with cans of Red Stripe and makeshift parties. Pick your groceries from Ridley Road market as the fishmonger smokes a defrosted vibrant blue aquatic creature and shopping carts of uncovered lamb carcasses make their way to the butcher's counter.

It ain't pretty – Dalston doesn't even have its own postcode. It's a transient destination for most, a precursor to settling down somewhere more 'family-friendly', like Walthamstow. Crucially, it's a real community drowned out as the council estates receive no funding – where its inhabitants are forever marginalised; where the disparity between the working and middle classes swells as more expensive, fancier spots open up. The raw materials of the town are knocked down and rebuilt as shiny objects. I should know. The estate I grew up in by Hackney Downs station no longer exists. My first primary school has changed its name twice over since I left. My favourite spot – the Blockbuster next to Mangal II – is now a bougie five-storey German-owned boutique hotel with its own brewery and influencer events. It's all a bit mad how it's changed. But it's home.

The neighbourhood is surrounded by Hackney, Newington Green, Shoreditch, Stoke Newington and Clapton, and it has a charm and appeal like no other. Racism and prejudices seem like abnormalities. Turkish, black and every other ethnic community meld in this flavourful melting pot, with a sprinkling of white (and mostly rich) seasoning. Embodying it all is a local council that, for all its faults (don't get me started), is impregnably left wing and progressive. A place everyone wants to be seen at, familiar with, tagged in. Often hailed as the world's coolest neighbourhood and a must-visit destination, Dalston is a hipster's rite of passage. A designer's stomping ground. A foodie's haunt. A junkie's territory. An LGBTQ+ safe space. When the 2011 London riots happened, the first port of resistance where Turkish business owners didn't allow kids to smash their windows. It made global news.

Walk. Explore. You won't count many families or young children. There are very few pushchairs and teenagers. Nor do you see a lot of the elderly. Very few forts are built here. Too noisy, too charged, too fast. Yet, and this is hard to ascertain why exactly, it really has a community feel. You know the local shopkeepers by their first name. You feel protective of your place at the local lido. You see a fancy new building and wince together in horror.

Mangal II is Dalston. It's historic and deep in craft and appeal yet modern, exciting and 'cool'. It's Turkish but very London. It is tattered and old; its tables are uneven, its woodchipped staircase exposed, its sign covered by the rear expressions of a pigeon. It has an energized dining room and a young, creative and multicultural team with an arsenal of flavourful dishes. Our restaurant could not be copy-pasted in another area in London and fit in quite as aptly. We're at the very beginning of the Turkish stretch of Stoke Newington Road (still in Dalston), and the spots become more traditional as you head towards Stoke Newington High Street, just as they become more commercialised and franchised in the opposite direction towards Shoreditch. We are delicately poised exactly where we belong. Behind the restaurant, there are gambling dens, drug deals, litter, illegal parking and vandalism. And bang in the middle of it all is a new build that was once a mechanics. But it all adds to the tapestry of this strange and unique pocket of London.

We love Dalston. Without it, we are a scorched piece of earth. Ocakbaşı burning with no mouths to feed, smouldering into embers and then ash. Disintegrating by smoke. A body without its soul. Dalston was our foray into London: for my parents, myself and my siblings. Our parents landed here as their first step in the UK, and we were born here. It's imperfect. It's problematic. It's strange, pretentious, unequal and ever-changing. It's dangerous and unfamiliar and local and ours. It's diluted and dirty and chic and edgy. It's everything and yet it's nothing. Like its high concentration of Turkish kebab houses, it's a lot of hot air. Not even a postcode. But it's home.

— Ferhat

Ferhat's Story

I was born in 1989, in a house in Dalston, three weeks premature – in the cold of winter, with the ambulance late to arrive and my parents living in what can best described as a squat. My mum's friend/ flatmate delivered me. 'Waaah! Waaah!' Those were the first sounds I presumably bellowed.

For my first two years of life, we moved constantly around Hackney – until the council provided us with permanent housing at an estate right by Hackney Downs station, where we would reside for another five years. Everyone I knew at that time was either Turkish, Kurdish or Nigerian. Our school was a world where our ethnicity was the primary identity; a sense of Britishness/Londoner was secondary. We were predominantly second-generation immigrants with parents who stayed within their communities and, by extension, playtime with friends meant a mishmash of broken Turkish and English, where neither language was mastered. In fact, I started reception at the age of four (I had bypassed nursery altogether because there wasn't availability for me), unable to speak a word of English, bar a few swears I'd picked up from the kids in the estate. One day at school, I pooped my underwear in the toilets and panicked; without knowing how to express a cry for help in English, I shouted 'NURSE!' continually for what felt like an eternity until an angel came to my rescue.

This is not an autobiography. It is about Mangal II. But it would be remiss of me to explain its story and evolution without my own. Beyond the glamour, the awards, the hype, the celeb hangouts, our Insta feed, the interviews, the Twitter account, the Munchies YouTube videos and the noise, there's a kid – born to and raised by truly hard-working parents. We lived on a ground-floor flat facing the tarmac we used as our playground/football pitch. Every day, from our kitchen window, my parents would hand out the left-over *lahmacun* from their first restaurant, Mangal I, to the kids in our social housing complex. It was like a scene from 'The Wire', except delicious Turkish flatbreads with lamb, onion and tomato paste were being pushed instead of crack cocaine. My Nigerian friends – their parents, too – became obsessed with lahmacun. It seemed such a generous act, but it was second nature for my mum. My dad would bring home all this food he couldn't bear to waste, and she would see that it went to happy homes. You see, both were raised in poverty. Sharing food was as natural a reflex to them as holding one's breath under water. There are no photographs documenting their generosity, no local gazette press releases, nothing – just the act itself and my word. But it happened. It happened with modesty and quietness because that's just what they did. They shared. They supported their neighbours. They looked out for one another, and it was the most normal, unspoken thing.

Just before my eighth birthday and seven months after Sertaç was born, we moved to Chingford on the outskirts of London, bordering Essex and embodying all the latter's conservative ideals. We made the move because our home was robbed... twice. As nostalgic as my memories are of growing up in Dalston, the violence and the danger were palpable – even for my tiny child world. My parents made the very common decision to raise their three children in the quiet suburbs. This includes my parents' first-born, my sister, Ayşegül, two years my elder – who I grew up with the most and whom I adore. My formative years were shared with her, and we both tried to acclimatise to our new surroundings. It's a move I almost wish they hadn't made.

The culture shock was real. Immediately, I felt like an outsider, an *other*. City concrete was replaced by endless green forests, where the mysterious woodlands, with their rustic nature and wild pastures, presented a foreign danger I felt unconditioned for. Friendships were hard to come by due to the cultural differences in our interactions. Structured play dates and their formalities were alien to my feral/untainted mind. We even stopped handing out lahmacun after we moved.

When I finally achieved social acceptance and had new friends come over to play FIFA, the immaculate Turkish dishes my mum would serve them would be met with repulsion. When the sweet peppers arrived, stuffed with meat and rice and onions in a light tomato broth (customers revel in a popular iteration of this dish to this day, page 206), the kids would flip out, visibly recoil and ask if we had any frozen pizza or chicken nuggets. It made me feel ashamed: ashamed of my culture, ashamed of my mum's exquisite cooking, ashamed of myself. I would be embarrassed to tell my classmates what my dad did for a living (he was the owner of Mangal II by this point) out of fear of being ridiculed and further excluded. I wished he worked in an office somewhere with a stupid tie and was available on weekends. In reality, he worked six and a half days a week. I only saw him on Sunday afternoons.

Everything I learned about being a boy or growing up, I figured out myself or looked up to older cousins (a load of wrong 'uns) for inspiration. But I grew tired of not seeing my dad. One Saturday morning, I blockaded the door to stop him from going to work without me. I remember it vividly. He looked at me like I was mad, then turned to my mum to see if I was serious. She knew how badly I missed him, how much I yearned to be in his presence. She said we could trial it and see how I got on, heading out with him to work from 12 p.m. until 12 a.m. And that's how it started.

Defeated, he reluctantly let me sit beside him in his big red Jeep as we made the pilgrimage from Chingford to Dalston via Lea Bridge Road. That was Saturday. And every Saturday for the next ten years.

...

There I was, eleven years old, pan-cooking chopped liver, kidneys and chicken breasts to unsuspecting punters in the restaurant's basement, away from prying eyes and child labour protection services. I loved it. I was paid £10 a week and built up my savings to buy video games and indulge a weirdly mature addiction to daily newspapers and football and gaming magazines. My love of restaurants and words and media and print were amalgamated. Oh, plus the hair wax – I bought so much hair wax. Look, it was between 2000 and 2005, and I was on a lifelong journey of desperately failing to impress girls.

Life was good. Sure, occasionally I'd have to babysit my dad as he'd have a lock-in with lots of drink, and I'd wait until the early hours for him to sober up or call a cab home. Without a mobile phone, tablet or other digital distractions to occupy my time, I'd sit alone with my thoughts with sheets of paper and a pen to amuse me. I'd draw and draw and draw. Maps. WWE wrestlers. Football best XIs. Batman logos. The creative output was good; however, the trauma of it all was impactful and would later emerge in life.

But I was happy enough. With the routine classes, work and biking with friends after school, I grew to call Chingford home. My childhood memories are relatively positive. And most of all, I really, and I mean REALLY, loved being at the restaurant. Over the next five years, I built a rapport with everyone. The staff's Turkish nickname for me, quite unfairly for a child, was 'Hey Useless' (like, 'Hey Arnold'). Customers saw me work my way up from the visible dining room of the restaurant, polishing plates and cutlery, to now running to clear tables. But, most importantly, my dad loved having me by his side and would open up about his absurd and tragic upbringing during our drives to and from work.

I loved the buzz and the theatre of the restaurant world. On weekdays, I was a kid. On weekends, I was a part of the ensemble. Every Saturday, I was on stage, holding conversations with grown-ups – it was formative for my social development.

When I was sixteen, my world turned upside down. That summer, I became skinnier and weaker. I tried to ignore the signs that my once athletic, strong, fit self was deteriorating. By October, during sixth form, my whole body shut down. I went from 9.5 stones (133 lbs) to 7.2 stones (100 lbs) – my frame shadowed a skeleton and my cheekbones screamed to crawl out of my hollow face. I was soon rushed to the hospital after a consultation with my GP, put on a drip and admitted into a ward with forty patients whose average age was seventy. I wasn't allowed to eat for six days and, worst of all, I didn't have a clue what was happening to me or how I had ended up in this cold room with sickness all around. Every night, there were howls of screams by elderly patients who fought death to the death. It was a living nightmare.

After many doctors' tests and endless injections, I was eventually diagnosed with Crohn's disease, a chronic inflammatory bowel condition. My life felt over. I didn't know what it would entail, but what transpired were seven operations over the next six years, each one chopping away at my bowels to get to the surgical root of the problem whilst strong medications and the occasional steroids tried to heal me simultaneously. I wore pads like a baby. Embarrassed, I kept this a secret from all my friends and my grand total of zero girlfriends. The humiliation ran deep and, worst of all, I had to have a new diet. No spicy foods, crunchy salads, alcohol, cigarettes, food with sharp edges that might impact one's stomach (like chopped carrot) or fiery qualities (like the burn of whisky). I ate like a baby, lived like a baby and felt like a baby throughout university and my early working life.

I still went to work. It was my escape from reality, and it helped me briefly forget my bodily failings and my emotional, crippling sadness at how my youth was stripped away from me whilst my peers lived unabashedly free and recklessly. I couldn't even eat much of what we sold, which was a double blow. I'd settle for lentil soups, mushy mezze like Aubergine Yogurt (page 44), pillowy pide bread (page 120) and warm mint teas. My body would roar in protest when I'd indulge in the occasional kebab. Worst of all, for two years, every time I went to the toilet, I would take two painkillers and lie down until the remedy hit because my bowels were in absolute agony. It wasn't fun, but I grew mentally resilient by the end of those hellish years. Pent up and looking to channel my pain whilst juggling a master's degree and working full-time at Mangal II, I took to Twitter under the restaurant's name and started tweeting dry, dark, satirical material. At the time, it was the first hospitality business to go off the beaten track with a funny and irreverent account, and it soon gained traction.

My family business needed improvements, but my dad resisted change and fought back at every suggestion. Frustrated, I began mocking our restaurant in a comic tone, leading our establishment to become busier and more loved. For every restaurant that tweeted about their great menu and service, I countered with silliness:

'Parents – rather than asking if we have "baby changing facilities" you should just accept your baby the way it is.'

'This city was good before all the bloody immigrants came here. Now it's the fucking best.'

'Customer: I'm gluten-free, vegan, lactose-intolerant, coeliac.
What do you recommend?
Me: Champagne – It's a fucking miracle you're alive! Let's celebrate!'

And so on. It gave the restaurant a new lease of life and brought a wave of new hipster customers who came for the irony and returned for the great food at great value (with a few subtle changes).

My dad didn't understand what I was expressing online but would touch base with me now and again. 'Son, are you still writing things online? Yeah? OK, good, keep it up. We're very busy. Also, stop swearing. I saw a lot of "Fucks".' I carried on tweeting, and the restaurant, whilst unremarkable and standardised in its offering, continued to trickle along and kept us all afloat.

...

During this time, I met my first girlfriend, who moved to London for me, just as I was completing my master's in International Economic Law, Justice and Development (LLM). I was amazed that someone could like and want to be with me, a man who was repulsed by his own body and felt as undesirable as a toilet brush. It was a revelation – especially someone as beautiful and funny as she was.

Life came at us fast. She (Fatime) was twenty-four; I was twenty-six. Before we both knew it, she was pregnant. Parenthood wasn't on the agenda, but our love and bond were so strong – blindly optimistic, we went for it. And I became a father to my son, Zeki (whose character and artistic lens inspire me every day).

By this point, my dad had retired from work. Sertaç was nineteen and doing an art foundation course. It was me, the restaurant and my young family – a world of responsibility bestowed upon a young man who had grown up relatively sheltered and ill.

The restaurant was also in a bad way – many of our staff were kind but untrained, uneducated and, occasionally, problematic. Managing a range of brutish personalities prone to skiving, stealing, sulking and scheming was an experience. I learned a lot, and my confidence grew as my role turned to one of a fireman, putting out flames of danger that could damage my business and my future every day.

Truthfully, though, I was coasting at work. I was dealing with manic staff and their endless personal problems, which kept seeping into work. And then there were countless spoilt and demanding customers accustomed to a world of freebies at little value because we were a kebab house – an expectation created by our peers in the industry. I tried to deal with these issues whilst pursuing creative endeavours outside of hospitality (simultaneously working social media jobs through my Twitter fame: freelancing at *Mail Online*, to my deep shame, and *Vice*, writing articles for *The Independent*, etc.). I never fully immersed myself in my role as a restaurant owner. I didn't cook. I didn't train or

stage anywhere. I didn't have industry peers. Frankly, I didn't know shit.
I inherited a mess, and through sheer force, I kept it from going under.
If the staff were crafty, I became wilier. If the occasional customers
tried to take advantage of Turkish/British kebab culture by insisting
on more and more discounts, freebies and larger portions, I grew
harder and unrelenting. If I didn't have pals in the scene, I became more
resolute with an outsider's attitude. My greatest attributes were my
hard work and charm on the service floor, plus my genuine interest
in food, wine and eating out.

I always aspired for more, for better. As did Sertaç. We spoke a
lot, especially during his stints at the restaurant before his formative
pilgrimage to Denmark, where he honed his craft (page 38). We wanted
Mangal II to be better: cleaner, lighter, punchier and more organised,
without the freebies or BYOB policy. We wanted to create and carry
ourselves with pride. But I didn't have the conviction to do it alone.

By this time, the restaurant had racked up its fair share of debt to
suppliers as we were squeezed by competitors offering more food for
less. We couldn't raise our prices, nor could we make a stand against
people bringing in their own drinks since every surrounding business
allowed it and offered similar menus. I also expanded my family during
this time, as Fatime and I became parents to our second child, our
daughter, Juno (the most charismatic human on this planet).

I felt more isolated as I took on more responsibility and struggled
alone to keep everything afloat. My world crumbled and, by the time
the pandemic struck, my marriage had broken down and my staff
had abandoned Mangal II. My future was unstable. And that's when
I made the call. I asked Sertaç to come home. He was ready to. The rest
is history.

— Ferhat

Sertaç's Story

I always found it hard to concentrate in secondary school. When I joined, it was compulsory to do a verbal and non-verbal exam to test our IQ – I scored so high that I'd managed my way into the 'Gifted and Talented' percentile. Shocking as, in the years that followed, I barely scraped Cs across the board. In truth, I did try but it was impossible for me to focus on a book for more than ten minutes. (We've figured out, in recent years, that the problem was, more than likely, ADHD.) All day, every day, all I wanted to do was practise my drums – I'd been drumming since I was seven and, by my teens, played in most bands in the area. I was also a decent illustrator, though my parents regarded these interests as hobbies and not professions.

I spent more time with my mum growing up as my dad was always at the restaurant, which was great until I was deemed a low-performing teenager. In my dad's absence, Mum would make up for the both of them in regard to discipline. I'd be banned from using my phone for weeks at a time. The internet router would be unplugged for hours each day. I'd be dragged to tutoring classes in hopes that something might sink in. My best friend, Sonny, and I sat through three (painfully long) hours a week with Ruth, a sweet and kind assistant head teacher who was fully aware that our parents were wasting their money. Sonny would arrive with nuggets of hash, and we'd get very high before each session. Ruth would enter the room and smirk at us, with our blood-shot eyes, then explain the principles of chemistry. To this day, when I see Sonny's mum and the topic of Ruth comes up, she begins with 'That poor woman...'

By the time I was fourteen, my mum had exhausted all of her disciplinary options. After one too many incidents she declared, no phone, no internet, no friends. I was to be at the restaurant on the weekends. And so, the sentencing era began. I was sent away to do hard time at Mangal II. How was I not supposed to associate kitchen work with punishment? I quickly resented the restaurant. I never understood why the smoking of a little weed in the suburbs was more harmful than placing me in Dalston, London's epicentre of crack and heroin.

Every Friday and Saturday night, I'd work different sections of the restaurant: front of house, back of house, KP. I was missing out on an integral part of my teenage development: whilst my friends were socialising and partying, I was running up and down the restaurant floor. Mangal II was loud, hot and fast – those evenings were crammed full of locals, politicians, musicians, actors and artists. The adrenaline was real. I would physically cringe at forced conversations with guests – we quickly realised I wasn't made for front of house. I was to prep vegetables, plate mezze, run food to the chefs and hand them their orders of skewered meats to grill.

Dad retired the year I joined, leaving the restaurant to be managed by Ferhat, who was running the floor with a mixed crew deriving from Turkey, Bulgaria, Turkmenistan, Austria and Morocco. Ferhat showed me the ropes, we'd enjoy a beer together at the end of a shift, and he'd explain the intricacies of the business. I'd return home by 1 a.m. and feel like a man. It felt like I skipped the classic coming-of-age story and fast-tracked into adulthood.

After I had a few unsuccessful stints at college and university, Ferhat convinced me to return to the restaurant to earn some money and begin my adult life. By twenty, I was a competent grill cook, running services on the grill most nights of the week and serving up to 150 guests an evening. I didn't have the chance to work with my dad before he retired, so I had to acquire knowledge from the other chefs at the restaurant – a crew of mostly Bulgarian chefs who weren't exactly interested in cooking itself, but more as a means to an end. Life wasn't going as planned: I felt like a jack of all trades and without purpose and exceptional attributes. I felt unimpressive.

The prompt for change happened two years into working full-time at Mangal II, when I made the decision to leave. Ferhat was supportive. He explained that the expectation of the restaurant operations was on him and he didn't want the same inhibitions on me. He encouraged me to go explore and move abroad; he held the fort. After much deliberation, I figured I could explore my creativity through food and still earn a living. I booked a one-way ticket to Copenhagen with no plan or work in place.

•••

I eventually applied for the internship program at Noma's sister restaurant 108, run by Kristian Baumann. I spent an entire afternoon crafting a heartfelt cover letter, had my siblings proofread it and sent it off. I got accepted.

Up until this point, I had never met another chef my age. I figured I'd have a competitive edge as I'd grown up in a restaurant. I arrived with a couple of Dick knives and a Masamoto slicer gifted to me by my sister from her honeymoon in Tokyo.

The three ensuing months were like a fever dream. I spent seventeen hours a day in a room – three days on, three days off – surrounded by the most talented and regimented people I'd ever met. I was out of my depth. I had to undo everything I thought was right: holding my knife, cleaning vegetables, scrubbing a work surface, positioning myself in the kitchen, moving swiftly. I was a chef de partie's (CDP) nightmare. I was brutalised. I would push to be better each day: I'd avoid the same mistakes from the day before and try to get on the good side of the chefs. The reality is first impressions last, and I had lost.

I stuck it out; the realities of this new world had to sink in. I'd have to adjust my perspective, have my wits about me and knuckle down to catch up to my peers.

I lined up a job at Slurp, a local ramen joint run by Niklas Harmsen and Philipp Inreiter, who was ex-Noma and had cooked in Japan. My goal was to work to a sufficient standard for my age. At Slurp, we sold up to 250 bowls of ramen each day and prepared 120 litres/127 quarts of stocks in massive bratt pans. Misos, kimchi and vegetables all required exacting preparations.

Jules St-Cyr and I had met at 108 in the internship program. We were the same age, but he was faster, tidier and more organised. To be fair, he ran circles around most people in that room. Above all, he had fantastic energy, and 108 soon offered him a job. After I'd left 108, we'd meet most nights after work for a beer and talk food. Those conversations drove me to push harder and to focus less on what my peers were doing – our talks kept me in the city and on the right track.

I moved onto Matt Orlando's new project, his dream brewery and my most prolific training ground, Broaden and Build. A massive warehouse complex – with giant industrial fermentation chambers and a brand-new kitchen – here was a place where everything clicked. As a small team, we had a lot of one-on-one time together and, in turn, I had access to a lot of information. There was the head chef, Elliot Bernardo, who was originally from Buffalo, New York. He was unpretentious, no bullshit and straight to the point. The job wasn't right until it was right. I liked that about him: there wasn't any ego in what he was doing. I had to just shut up, listen and do the job properly. Today, I consider him one of my closest friends. There was also Kim Wejendorp, Amass and Broaden and Build's R&D chef, a towering, hyper-intelligent chef from New Zealand. He was a fountain of knowledge if he considered you worthy (which I wasn't for the first nine months I was there). Sous Chef Orlando Ribeiro was a charismatic wild card from Portugal, a Dairy alumni who was nicknamed Tornado. He ran around nonstop. I'd watch him scrub floors so hard you'd think the objective was to scrape off a layer of concrete each time. He came equipped with tips and tricks from his London days. He was a beast.

Matt's zero-waste approach was heavily applied here, and we would spare nothing. We built layers of flavour from things that would typically go in the bin in your average kitchen. Leftover cream and milk would make cultured creams and crème fraîche. Vegetable trims would be fermented and powdered for seasonings. Kim would be constantly working on projects, such as converting old fridges into blackening chambers and making deliciousness from spent beer grains. It was amazing to practise this approach day in and day out. It has been one of the most rewarding working experiences I've ever had – I was part of an all-star team, learning from the best.

I reached a stage where I felt like a machine: I was clean, organised and prepared. A couple months had gone by without being told off or yelled at. I felt like I finally understood the role of a high-functioning CDP. Elliot would talk to me more frankly and as an equal. He'd trust me with more jobs, show me more techniques beyond my section and ask me to problem solve when things were going south. He'd let me work on my own projects, which sometimes made it to the menu.

Everything was great until one rainy day in November, when I had overslept. I felt anxiety, adrenaline and nausea all at once. Here I was, preparing for a berating for the first time in months. All my hard work for nothing, a lamb to the slaughter. I got on my bike and blasted through the torrential rain; the twenty-minute cycle felt like an age. I arrived soaking wet and out of breath. Before I had the chance to apologise, Elliot instructed me to go and get changed. When I stepped outside, Elliot approached from the pass. 'I went through your notebook to see what you had to do today. It's so organised,' he said. 'Your notes are clean, detailed and easy to decipher. You've made a massive improvement. Well done.'

I was in shock. I was prepared for a beat-down for showing up late but, instead, I was praised for my organisational skills. For the first time in my cooking career, I felt vindicated. I was entering a new phase. I had all the energy to take it to the next level, planning my next moves... completely unaware we were moving towards a global lockdown.

— Sertaç

Page 40
From top, clockwise:
Sertaç at Slurp; at Broaden and Build, grilled lamb shoulder; the team at 108; tomatoes from Birkemosegaard Farm.

Page 41
From top, clockwise:
Foraged ceps, Sertaç standing next to a Douglas pine at Gribskov forest; Bnb's forager with hen of the woods at Amass.

Aubergine Yogurt

Serves 4–6

2 aubergines (eggplants)
1 Kapya pepper or red bell pepper
Sunflower oil, for brushing
400 g (14 oz/1¾ cups) Turkish
   or Greek yogurt
2 cloves garlic, minced
2½ teaspoons fine salt
1¼ teaspoons Aleppo chilli flakes
1½ teaspoons dried mint
1½ tablespoons extra-virgin olive oil
2 teaspoons lemon juice
Warm bread and grilled meats,
   to serve

Preheat a charcoal grill over high heat until the coals are white hot. Add the whole aubergines (eggplants) directly onto the coals and grill for 20 minutes, until all sides are charred. Brush the pepper with sunflower oil and grill over a grate for 3 minutes on each side. Transfer the vegetables to a large bowl, then cover with clingfilm (plastic wrap). Set aside for 30 minutes to steam. Peel the skins, then remove the stems and seeds. Finely chop both.

In a bowl, combine the aubergines, peppers and the remaining ingredients and mix well. Refrigerate for 1 hour.

Serve chilled with warm bread and grilled meats.

Ezme

Ezme improves with time when the ingredients have had a chance to marinate in their own juices. If you prefer it sharp with greater acidity, then serve it immediately. Otherwise, leave it for a day or two in the refrigerator to develop the flavours.

This dish works best in late summer when tomatoes and peppers are well ripened. *Ezme* means 'to crush' in Turkish, so it's important that all the ingredients are well chopped.

Serves 2–4

2 tomatoes, finely chopped
50 g/1¾ oz Kapya or red bell
  pepper, seeded, deveined
  and finely chopped
1 Sivri pepper (50 g/1¾ oz),
  finely chopped
1½ tablespoons finely
  chopped parsley
1 tablespoon finely chopped
  red onion
1½ teaspoons fine salt
½ teaspoon sweet pepper flakes
  (*tatlı pul biber*)
½ teaspoon sumac
½ teaspoon dried mint
½ teaspoon dried purple basil
  (*reyhan*)
4 teaspoons *salgam* (page 157)
4 teaspoons pomegranate molasses
4 teaspoons olive oil
2 teaspoons lemon juice

In a bowl, combine the tomatoes, peppers, parsley and onion and mix well. Stir in the remaining ingredients.

Transfer to a serving plate and serve at room temperature.

Cold Aubergine Ezme

Derived from the classic mezze *patlıcan ezme,* this dish combines smoky aubergine (eggplant), sharp lemon and fresh garlic for the perfect end-of-summer side dish. Resting it in the refrigerator will enhance the texture.

Serves 2–4

2 large aubergines (eggplants)
1 Kapya pepper or red bell pepper
2 cloves garlic, minced
3 tablespoons white wine vinegar
1 tablespoon lemon juice
1 tablespoon finely chopped parsley
1½ teaspoons fine salt
1 teaspoon garlic powder
½ teaspoon black pepper
Extra-virgin olive oil, for drizzling

Preheat a charcoal grill over high heat until the coals are white hot. Add the aubergines (eggplants) and pepper and grill for 10 minutes, until all sides are charred. Transfer the vegetables to a large bowl, then cover with clingfilm (plastic wrap). Set aside for 30 minutes to steam. Peel the skins, then remove the stems and seeds.

Finely chop the aubergines and pepper. (Do not leave any large chunks.) Place in a bowl, then mix in the remaining ingredients except the olive oil.

Add enough olive oil to submerge the ezme. Cool in the refrigerator, then serve.

Yogurt with Cucumber and Mint

Serves 2–4

½ small cucumber
250 g (9 oz/1¼ cups) Turkish
   or Greek yogurt
1 clove garlic
1 teaspoon fine salt
1 teaspoon lemon juice
½ teaspoon dried mint
Good-quality extra-virgin olive oil,
   for drizzling
Crusty bread, to serve

Peel the cucumber so equal parts of skin and flesh are visible. Cut into 5-mm/¼-inch cubes.

Put the yogurt into a large bowl. Grate in the garlic. Fold in the cucumbers and the remaining ingredients except the olive oil and mix well.

Drizzle the olive oil on top, then serve with crusty bread.

Braised Spinach in Yogurt

Serves 4–6

1½ tablespoons sunflower oil
⅓ onion, thinly sliced
3 cloves garlic
400 g/14 oz spinach leaves
Pinch of fine salt, plus
    1¼ tablespoons
400 g (14 oz/1¾ cups) Turkish
    or Greek yogurt
1 tablespoon lemon juice
2 teaspoons white pepper
2 teaspoons Aleppo chilli flakes
Good-quality extra-virgin olive oil,
    for drizzling
Warm bread, to serve

Heat the sunflower oil in a large frying pan over medium-high heat. Add the onions and sauté for 5 minutes, until softened and translucent. Thinly slice 2 cloves of garlic. Add the garlic and sauté for another minute, until fragrant. Add the spinach and a pinch of salt and sauté for another 3 minutes, until just wilted. Remove the pan from the heat.

Finely chop the remaining garlic clove. Add it to the pan, then stir in the yogurt and lemon juice. Season with 1¼ tablespoons of salt, the white pepper and chilli flakes. Transfer to a serving bowl, then cover with clingfilm (plastic wrap).

Serve at room temperature or chilled, drizzled with olive oil and with warm bread.

Tomato and Walnut Salad

Serves 2–4

2–3 tomatoes, sliced
1 small red onion (75 g/2¾ oz), sliced
1 Sivri pepper (50 g/1¾ oz), julienned
½ cucumber, sliced
50 g (1¾ oz/scant 1 cup) chopped
    parsley
50 g (1¾ oz/½ cup) walnuts, toasted
1½ teaspoons sea salt
1½ teaspoons Aleppo chilli flakes
1½ teaspoons sumac
1¼ teaspoons dried mint
½ teaspoon dried purple basil
    (*reyhan*)
2½ tablespoons olive oil
2½ tablespoons pomegranate
    molasses
4 teaspoons lemon juice
Grilled meat, to serve (optional)

Combine all the ingredients in a large bowl. Mix well.

Serve alone as a mezze or with grilled meat, if desired.

Grilled Onion Salad

Our dad would grill the onions to order, dress them on a large chopping (cutting) board and send them out immediately, ripping hot. It's a classic Mangal II technique and a delicious accompaniment to grilled meats.

Serves 8

For the onions
4 large brown onions,
    each cut into 6 wedges
Olive oil, for brushing
Fine salt, for sprinkling

For the seasoning
100 g (3½ oz/1¾ cups)
    chopped parsley
2 teaspoons sea salt
2 teaspoons Aleppo chilli flakes
2 teaspoons sumac
1 teaspoon dried purple basil
    (*reyhan*)
2½ tablespoons
    pomegranate molasses
4 teaspoons lemon juice
4 teaspoons olive oil

Onions Preheat a charcoal grill over high heat until the coals are white hot.

Skewer 3 onion wedges onto a thick skewer. Make 7 more. Brush the onions with the oil and season with salt.

Place the skewers on the hot grill. Grill for 10 minutes on each side, until charred. (Use a rack if you have trouble balancing them on the grill.) Transfer the onions to a bowl.

Seasoning Combine all the ingredients in a bowl and mix well.

Assembly Combine the onions and the seasoning and marinate for 5 minutes. Transfer to a serving bowl and serve immediately.

Lentil Soup

I serve this soothing, autumnal soup both at the restaurant and at home. My favourite accompaniment is a grilled cheese toastie, made with kashkaval cheese.

Serves 10–12

2 tablespoons vegetable oil
1 onion, finely chopped
1 carrot, finely chopped
150 g (5½ oz/⅔ cup) dried red lentils
400 ml (14 fl oz/1⅔ cups) white wine
100 g (3½ oz/scant ½ cup) Turkish
    tomato paste (*domates salçası*)
    or tomato purée (paste)
100 g (3½ oz/scant ½ cup) roasted
    pepper purée (*biber salçası*)
    or tomato purée (paste)
4 teaspoons sweet pepper flakes
    (*tatlı pul biber*)
4 teaspoons ground cumin
2 teaspoons black pepper
1½ tablespoons dried oregano
3 L (102 fl oz/12¾ cups) chicken
    or vegetable stock
300 g (7½ oz/1¼ cups) Turkish
    or Greek yogurt
4 cloves garlic, minced
Salt, to taste
Lemon juice, to taste

Heat the oil in a large stockpot over medium heat. Add the onions and sauté for 5 minutes, until they start to brown. Add the carrots and sauté for another 5 minutes, until caramelized. (Normally, garlic is added at this stage, but we add it later as Turkish food celebrates strong aromatic and acidic flavours.)

Add the lentils and sauté for 3–4 minutes, until slightly toasted. (We will add the salt later since it will draw out the liquid – thus, flavour.) Deglaze the lentils with 200 ml (7 fl oz/scant 1 cup) of wine. Stir in the purées and cook for 5 minutes, until fragrant. Add the spices and cook for another minute. Deglaze with the remaining 200 ml (7 fl oz/scant 1 cup) of wine and mix well.

Pour in the stock and bring to a boil. Reduce the heat to medium-low and simmer for 45 minutes–1 hour, depending on your desired lentil texture. Stir in the yogurt and garlic. Season with salt and lemon juice.

Left-over soup can be frozen in an airtight container for up to 3 months.

Shepherd's Salad

Serves 2–4

2 vine-ripened tomatoes, cut into
    1-cm/½-inch cubes
1 cucumber, cut into 1-cm/
    ½-inch cubes
1 onion, cut into 1-cm/½-inch pieces
4 teaspoons lemon juice
Fine salt, to taste
2 tablespoons finely chopped parsley
1½ tablespoons dried mint
2 teaspoons sweet pepper flakes
    (*tatlı pul biber*)
4 teaspoons olive oil
2 teaspoons pomegranate molasses
Grilled meats and mezze, to serve
Grated feta, for sprinkling (optional)

In a bowl, combine the tomatoes, cucumbers, onions, lemon juice and salt. Mix well. Add the remaining ingredients and mix again.

Serve alongside grilled meats and mezze or enjoy on its own with feta, if desired.

Filo Triangles

Serves 4

1 tablespoon sunflower oil,
  plus extra for frying
4 tablespoons finely chopped onions
2 cloves garlic, minced
300 g/10½ oz Turkish feta
  (*beyaz peynir*), crumbled
2 tablespoons finely chopped parsley
2½ teaspoons dried mint
1 teaspoon Aleppo chilli flakes
Salt, to taste
Lemon juice, to taste
1 (270-g/9¾-oz) pack filo pastry
1 egg, beaten

Heat the oil in a small frying pan over medium heat. Add the onions and garlic and sauté for 5 minutes, until the onions are translucent.

In a small bowl, combine the onion-garlic mixture, feta, parsley, mint and chilli flakes. Season with salt and/or lemon juice.

Lay out the filo pastry onto a clean work counter. Slice lengthwise into 10-cm/4-inch-wide strips.

Add a tablespoon of cheese filling at the top of the filo sheet and fold over the corner to make a triangle. Continue to fold, keeping the triangle shape intact. Once you reach the end of the pastry, brush the last flap of filo with the beaten egg and close. Set aside. Repeat with the remaining filo and filling.

Heat the oil to a depth of 2.5 cm/1 inch in a large frying pan to a temperature of 160°C/325°F. Working in batches to avoid overcrowding, carefully lower the pastries into the hot oil. Fry each side for 1½–2 minutes, until golden brown. Transfer to a paper towel–lined plate to drain. Set aside for 3 minutes, then serve.

Adana-Style Lamb Skewers

The key here is to create ridges in the köfte before it's grilled. Once cooked, it'll have different textures along the skewer – some juicier, others crispier.

While minced (ground) lamb, with 25% fattiness, can be used in this recipe, my preference is for a combination of freshly ground lamb shoulder and lamb fat. It contains less water than mince, allowing the köfte to stick to the skewer better.

Serves 6–8

750 g/1 lb 10 oz lean lamb shoulder,
    cut into 5-cm/2-inch cubes
250 g/9 oz lamb fat, cut into
    5-cm/2-inch cubes
1 Kapya or red bell pepper, seeded,
    deveined and finely chopped
4 teaspoons ground cumin
4 teaspoons salt
2 teaspoons sweet pepper flakes
    (*tatlı pul biber*)

To serve
Store-bought or home-made Pide
    (page 120)
Grilled vegetables
Sliced onions
Chopped parsley
Ground cumin, for dipping
Dried oregano, for dipping

Freeze the lamb shoulder and fat for 1 hour.

Mince the fat through the coarse setting of a meat grinder. Combine the lamb fat and shoulder in a bowl and mix well. Pass the mixture through the grinder, breaking down the fat enough so that the meat sticks to the skewer. Put the ground mixture into a metal bowl, then add the remaining ingredients and mix until it's uniform in colour. Refrigerate for 2–4 hours, until cold.

Weight out the mixture into 70-g/2½-oz portions and roll into balls. With damp hands, skewer one portion onto flat skewers. Wrap your hand around a skewer and clench into a fist to flatten the mixture, about 20 cm/8 inches in length. Then, using your thumb, make indentations along the meat to create the classic köfte shape. Repeat with the remaining skewers. Refrigerate until needed.

Preheat a charcoal grill over high heat until the coals are white hot. Add the skewers and grill for 2 minutes on each side, until sealed. Reduce the heat to medium and grill for another 3 minutes on each side, until caramelized.

To serve, place the bread on a platter. Top with the skewers and serve with the vegetables, onions, parsley, cumin and oregano.

Beyti

Similar to the Adana-Style Lamb Skewers (page 64), this beloved köfte is larger, spicier and garlicky. Wrap it in *lavaş* (Turkish balloon bread) and top with lashings of garlic yogurt and tomato-y halep sauce.

Serves 10

750 g/1 lb 10 oz lean lamb shoulder,
    cut into 5-cm/2-inch cubes
250 g/9 oz lamb fat, cut into
    5-cm/2-inch cubes
6 cloves garlic, minced
1 Kapya or red bell pepper, seeded,
    deveined and finely chopped
6 tablespoons finely chopped parsley
4 teaspoons fine salt
4 teaspoons ground cumin
2 teaspoons Aleppo chilli flakes

To serve
Store-bought or home-made Pide
    (page 120)
Grilled vegetables
Sliced onions
Chopped parsley
Dried oregano, for dipping
Ground cumin, for dipping

Freeze the lamb shoulder and fat for 1 hour.

Mince the fat through the coarse setting of a meat grinder. Combine the lamb shoulder and fat in a bowl and mix well. Pass the mixture through the grinder, breaking down the fat enough so that the meat sticks to the skewer. Put the ground mixture into a metal bowl, then add the remaining ingredients and mix until it's uniform in colour. Refrigerate for 2–4 hours, until cold.

Weigh out the mixture into 100-g/3½-oz portions and roll into balls. With damp hands, skewer one portion onto flat skewers. Wrap your hand around a skewer and clench into a fist to flatten the mixture, about 20 cm/8 inches in length. Then, using your thumb, make indentations along the meat to create the classic köfte shape. Repeat with the remaining skewers. Refrigerate until needed.

Preheat a charcoal grill over high heat until the coals are white hot. Add the skewers and grill for 2 minutes on each side, until sealed. Reduce the heat to medium and grill for another 3 minutes on each side, until caramelized.

To serve, place the pide on a platter. Top with the skewers and serve with the vegetables, onions, parsley, oregano and cumin.

Chicken Shish

Serves 4

100 g (3½ oz/½ cup) Turkish tomato
    paste (*domates salçası*) or tomato
    purée (paste)
100 g (3½ oz/scant ½ cup) Turkish
    or Greek yogurt
3½ tablespoons sunflower oil
4 teaspoons salt
2 teaspoons Aleppo chilli flakes
2 teaspoons white pepper
2 teaspoons ground cumin
1 kg/2 lbs 4 oz skinless, boneless
    chicken breasts, cut into
    3-cm/1¼-inch cubes

To serve
Grilled vegetables
Sumac onions
Store-bought or home-made Pide
    (page 120)

In a large bowl, combine all the ingredients except the chicken. Mix well. Fold in the chicken. Cover with clingfilm (plastic wrap) and refrigerate for 12 hours to marinade.

Skewer the chicken onto 4 thick skewers. Refrigerate, uncovered, for 2–3 hours to set the shape.

Preheat a charcoal grill over medium-high heat until the coals are white hot. Add the chicken skewers and grill for 10 minutes, turning occasionally, until all sides are caramelized and slightly charred. Set aside for 5 minutes, until the chicken reaches an internal temperature of 75°C/167°F.

Transfer to a serving platter and serve with vegetables, sumac onions and pide.

Chop Shish

Chop shish, or *çöp şiş,* is like a classic lamb shish but smaller and crispier. *Çöp,* meaning 'rubbish' in Turkish, originates from using all the scrap pieces of lamb to ensure nothing is wasted. Arguably better than the original shish.

Serves 4

1 kg/2 lbs 4 oz lean lamb shoulder, large pieces of fat reserved
4 tablespoons Turkish or Greek yogurt
3 tablespoons Turkish tomato paste (*domates salçası*) or tomato purée (paste)
3 tablespoons Turkish pepper paste (*biber salçası*)
2 tablespoons sunflower oil
4 teaspoons salt
2 teaspoons Aleppo chilli flakes
2 teaspoons ground cumin
2 teaspoons black pepper

To serve
Sumac onions
Grilled vegetables
Store-bought or home-made Pide (page 120)

Cut the lamb shoulder into 4 x 3-cm/1½ x 1¼-inch pieces. Place it into a bowl.

In a separate bowl, combine the remaining ingredients except the fat. Add the lamb and mix well. Cover with clingfilm (plastic wrap) and refrigerate for 12 hours.

Slice the fat into 2 x 3-cm/¾ x 1¼-inch pieces. Divide the lamb mixture into 8 portions. Skewer each piece lengthwise, alternating with pieces of fat (for a juicier and crispier texture combination). Refrigerate for 2–4 hours.

Preheat a charcoal grill over high heat until the coals are white hot. Add the skewers and grill for 4 minutes on each side until charred. Reduce the heat to medium and grill for another 4 minutes on each side, until cooked through. The aim is to char the meat but retain its juiciness inside.

Serve hot with sumac onions, vegetables and pide.

Falafel

Serves 4–6

500 g (1 lb 2 oz/2¼ cups) dried
   chickpeas
4 cloves garlic
1 small white onion
50 g/1¾ oz parsley
10 g/¼ oz coriander (cilantro)
1 tablespoon fine salt
1 tablespoon ground cumin
½ tablespoon black pepper
½ tablespoon ground coriander
¾ teaspoon Aleppo chilli flakes
¾ teaspoon paprika
2½ tablespoons plain
   (all-purpose) flour
2 teaspoons lemon juice
2 L (68 fl oz/8½ cups) sunflower oil,
   for deep-frying
Lemon wedges, to serve
Cacik (page 160) or Turkish
   or Greek yogurt, to serve

Put the chickpeas in a large bowl and add enough water to cover. Soak them overnight. Drain well.

In a food processor, combine the chickpeas, garlic, onion, parsley and coriander (cilantro). Pulse until coarsely ground. (Alternatively, pass the ingredients through a meat grinder as we do at the restaurant.) Mix in the spices. Add the flour and lemon juice and stir until the mixture begins to bind.

Heat the oil in a deep fryer or deep pan to 170°C/340°F. Roll the mixture into 50-g/1¾-oz balls. Working in batches to avoid overcrowding, carefully lower the falafel into the hot oil and deep-fry for 3–4 minutes, until golden. Using a slotted spoon, transfer falafel to a paper towel–lined plate to drain.

Serve warm with lemon wedges and yogurt.

Cooked falafels can be stored in an airtight container in the freezer for up to 3 months. To serve, defrost and re-fry.

Albanian-Style Livers

Serves 6

700 g/1 lb 9 oz lamb livers
700 ml (23 fl oz/scant 3 cups) milk
1 tablespoon sunflower oil
1 small onion, thinly sliced
150 g (5¼ oz/1¼ cups) plain
   (all-purpose) flour
5 tablespoons butter
3½ tablespoons dried oregano
2½ tablespoons ground cumin
1½ tablespoons Aleppo chilli flakes

To serve
Sumac onions
Parsley
Lemon wedge
Thick bread

Place the livers in a bowl of iced water for 12 hours to draw out any blood.

Drain the livers, then slice them into 2-cm/¾-inch cubes. Place them in a large bowl and add the milk. Cover and refrigerate for 6–12 hours.

Heat the oil in a frying pan over high heat. Add the sliced onions and sauté for 3 minutes, until they begin to caramelize.

Meanwhile, place the flour into a shallow bowl. Drain the lamb livers completely, then toss them in the flour. Add the livers and butter to the pan and sauté for 5 minutes, until caramelized. Remove the pan from the heat, then stir in the oregano, chilli flakes and cumin.

Serve with the sumac onions topped with the parsley, lemon wedge and bread to mop up the juices.

TRANSFORMATION
Original Dishes after Lockdown

By 2020, ten more Turkish restaurants had popped up within a 150-metre/165-yard radius – all boasting variations of the same menu. The restaurant was being undercut in price by local purveyors, and BYOB was a big part of the dining experience at joints in our spend category. Food sales aren't as profitable as one might believe, and restaurants rely heavily on the sale of drinks (wet sales) to make any kind of profit margin. We were implementing lunch and takeaway deals and offering free mezze on arrival, but it was a race to the bottom.

We were in debt, preparing food that lacked the same spark our dad had once served, and something needed to change. Mangal II needed to be an authentic representation of our own experiences rather than a bad rendition of our dad's offerings. The aim was to showcase the vibrancy of Turkish cooking and that it was a cuisine worthy of respect. We came to realise that our mission to showcase a new style of eating wasn't all that different to our father's plight of introducing ocakbaşı-style cooking to the UK thirty years ago (under the same roof AND the same name, no less). Somehow, we had to retain the same energy of the old restaurant without displeasing the regulars.

The goal was to save the business and have a healthier relationship with our workplace. But through word of mouth and some very important reviews, it became much more than that. Mangal 2.0 was born.

— Sertaç

Recipes

You Go to Work

When the world shuts down and society caves into a deep slumber, when every door is bolted and streets deserted – where do you go?

You go to work.

You enter an empty building, one you've spent more time in than any other in your life. Your home from home. The place you'd work a Saturday job (for a tenner) at the age of eleven. The same spot where you learned about dining customs and made lifelong friends and enemies of anonymous online reviewers. The very place you bonded with your father because the man just couldn't come home at a reasonable hour of day; so you would force yourself to spend as much time inside that building as possible – to remind yourself of the paternal figure in your life.

Here, the rickety old stairs and the storage cupboards wouldn't look out of place in a documentary about hoarders. A building where up to 150 people would come in to dine on a Saturday, a concoction of laughter and skewers slamming against the ocakbaşı and wine bottles opening for a gasp of air and the playlist blaring that you feel weirdly possessive over. But now empty and silent, like the aftermath of a nuclear war fifteen years later. A ghost town, a haunted house. The silence in Dalston was deafening. No sirens. No bar-dwellers. Just a few masked people quietly scrambling for loo roll and sanitiser.

You go to work every day because it's the only place where you find peace. It's just you and your brother, who returned home from Copenhagen at the beginning of the pandemic to face whatever dystopic horrors awaited, to the ones he loved most: his family. You pick him up from the airport and you touch base about life, your fears, your relationships, the general demise of the world as we know it, but the conversation is dominated by one topic: changing Mangal II.

The drive from Heathrow to north-east London changed everything. You decide in that forty-five-minute journey (the roads are empty, remember) to tear up the script, burn it to the ground and gut the whole fucking place. Make it your own. With a mountain of debt to suppliers and knackered apparatus. With no money, no staff (they all left to find jobs in supermarkets and takeaway joints) and not a single backer or believer. You do it anyway, because everything is already heading south – how could it get any worse?

You go to work every day, just the two of you. He asserts that we need to clean every single object in the restaurant before we do anything else. I look at him like a stranger, even though he's right. '*Everything?!*' Everything. Who is this person who left London as a care-free young cook and returns from Copenhagen military-hardened and systematic with a work ethic that makes me feel like Van Wilder? It takes me a while to get with the program, but we're invested and have no alternatives. Put up or shut up. We clash but I get scrubbing and he gets scraping.

At the beginning of the pandemic, we spend ten hours day in and day out cleaning every plate, table leg, knife, water jug (pitcher), floor tile. Our wrists become inflamed from all the vigorous repetitive motion. Sertaç's skin burns up from all the chemicals. We hardly have a penny to spend because the concept of government grants is still a pipe dream. We work, and we buy M&S bacon, Lurpak butter, nice bread and Tabasco and make little rolls to get us through the day. It feels a bit fancy, like we're eating out.

This is our survival – what rationing means to us spoilt kiddos. There are no bombs, but death is around us daily. He dies, she dies. Vulnerable people we know, even our relatives, drop like flies. To go to work is to further expose ourselves to that risk when we could be at home instead: watching TV, taking up baking, reading neglected novels on the dusty shelf or any other hellish escape for two adrenaline-fuelled workaholics. But the truth is it's not even a debate.
You go to work.

— Ferhat

The Second; the Third

And bang! You put your heart and soul into the relaunch of Mangal II in July 2020. After a three-month lockdown, which felt like an eternity, life begins again. Society peers out from the blinds of their windows. Feet trickle the pavement. Socially distanced conversations between loved ones at front doors are now replaced with embraces and hugs. The ocakbaşı is lit, and customers arrive with genuine excitement at the ecstatic prospect of having somebody else cook, serve and clean up after them. This is a luxury longed for during COVID-19's imprisonment.

Mangal II was on a voyage of discovery, returning from the nadir with a short, thoughtful menu, combining the best of its past – the return of hummus now home-made with soaked and grilled chickpeas (page 106) and a pide bread prepared with a sourdough starter that's dipped into olive oil before its literal baptism of fire (page 120) – with the revelatory new. We introduced the Mushroom Manti (page 162), Courgette Fritters with Sucuk Mayo (page 114) and Okra with Sucuk Jam (page 112).

We were growing by the week and gaining confidence with every tweak, validated by the positive feedback and overwhelming hype. The rust was wearing off, and we were near match fitness after months of no service and minimal human interaction. All the risks we took were slowly being rewarded, one bounce-back loan repayment at a time.

By November of 2020, with Covid cases rising, there was a second brief lockdown. By the time it arrived, we were exhausted and welcomed the break. Unlike most places, we didn't want to entertain the prospect of remaining open for takeaway. Everyone needed that little breather, knowing full well that when we returned as a fully functioning restaurant, expectations would be on overdrive. Instead, we rested, preserved our energy and itched for our return to service with customers dining in. We reopened, knowing that an inevitable third lockdown was around the corner, like the dying days of a relationship with a breakup unavoidable. We worked mournfully. The government seemed to only reopen between the second and third lockdown to boost the economy in time for Christmas – it felt very ill-thought and dangerous to society and our industry. And then the dreaded day came. Unlike the second lockdown, where murmurings of a festive reopening gave us hope of carrying on, the third one was the abyss – with no certainties, no return in sight.

Time to get creative.

Though rarely discussed, the third lockdown lasted the longest: December 2020 to May 2021. We couldn't afford another break, and neither could our staff. Furlough payments would not cover basic living costs, and we owed it to our team, our families and our wonderful and loyal patrons to run as a takeaway business until our holy resurrection as a dine-in restaurant come spring (unbeknownst to us that it would take that long at the time).

Whilst our menu – with all of its flavour bombs – was an absolute hit with eat-in guests, not every dish was replicable in a takeaway format. You cook and package the food, it's picked up by delivery driver, sometimes late, and then it is delivered to the customer's home. But with muddled journeys, confusing road maps, eight-storey walk-ups to some flats, the contents – once finally plated – can be cold, sad and gloomy. Many variables work against the most important conclusion: taste and satisfaction. We adhered to a delivery system regardless. And believe me, there'd be mishaps daily and refunds accordingly. But the real fun was in our on-the-go offerings.

Being seasoned lockdown veterans, our average customers threw caution to the wind and wanted to get out and about. If the Prime Minister was having lock-ins and his Svengali was driving up and down the country, you could sure bet that East Londoners simply had had enough and wanted to maintain a social life. Everyone was after a takeaway sandwich of great quality, beer on tap in plastic cups and lots of park get-togethers with friends. And at Mangal II we were aware of this strong need. So we worked with Partizan Brewery to serve their superlative lager, IPA and pale ale. We prepared pide sandwiches, which were absolute showstoppers. It kept us afloat, our staff busy (and more importantly, paid), our landlord off our backs and our morale high. It saved us.

What was so great about the food? Daily-made *yaprak döner* in a thick Turkish pide with sumac onions, chilli and garlic sauce at £8. Grilled line-caught mackerel fillets with a burst of dill mayo and sandwiched between pide for £8. We were like the fishermen and women of Istanbul's Galata Bridge, catching and cooking the fish in sarnies and selling them to passers-by. Herbaceous, life-affirming fried falafels were prepared downstairs and shown compassion by grilled preserved pickled red peppers, sweet yet sharp, all enveloped in fresh bread. £7. These three superheroes rescued us and the public. We'd sell over a hundred sandwiches a day. We worked like an assembly line. There was joy and harmony in our movements, in our exchanges with the punters at the door, in our lives. We had a purpose every day.

The pides received a lot of coverage and acclaim and kept us in the restaurant lexicon for the foreseeable future. We proved that we weren't a one-trick pony, that we were versatile and adaptable to change. Whatever the government wanted to impose on a small, family-run business, we were ready – bolstered by a loyal team, a devoted customer base and a raging fire inside our bellies and on our ocakbaşı.

Still, the third lockdown pushed us to our limits. There's only so much you can make from selling sandwiches and takeaway deliveries. The gas bills, the rent, the wages, the suppliers' fees, the repair costs – they remained. We were pushed to the brink financially, with no backers and no external support, bar a measly few thousand the government offered (£4000 may be a lot to hand to an individual, but it's a pittance for a London restaurant). Only our ingenuity and hard work would pull us out of this slump. Even then, every month we were on the verge of going bust. With battered equipment and a fragile building structure (we had to install a new staircase to replace the shattered steps that led into the kitchen), we took out a bank loan and extended our overdraft to stay afloat.

Writing these words brings back a flash of PTSD. The adrenaline of swimming against the tide and not drowning, of beating the force from the elements and emerging victorious is not as comforting as the stress and worry it all induced. There are battle scars in our walls. Recognising the fragility of our livelihood, and how quickly it can be taken away, is not something you get over in a hurry. Who would have predicted a global pandemic? Who would have prepared for society coming to a collapse? Who would have entered the void in December 2020 and known it would last five months? The human spirit is resilient and proactive, but the forces of nature (and government) are relentless and merciless. But we got through it.

We reopened in May as an actual restaurant. It was a relief. Our first decision? No more takeaway! We were eternally grateful that it allowed us to be productive and test new flavour combinations, which brought a confidence to our new dishes. After experiencing success during the final lockdown, Sertaç came armed with a menu that was delectably immersive and out there with undertones of familiarity. The transformation is all there if you visit our Instagram profile; you'll bear witness to the evolution of the dishes from July 2020 through until May 2021, and then the outburst of creativity that followed thereafter for in-house dining.

We are still asked about that Mackerel Pide (page 124), the most popular of the lot. When the tragic earthquake struck Syria and Turkey in 2023, killing tens of thousands of our countrymen, women and children, we had to act. What could we offer, besides something monetary, to help rebuild an ancient and historic land that had been obliterated by decades of poor building regulations and a disregard for human life over backhanded construction deals? With donations from our friends – mackerel by Fin and Flounder and focaccia by

The Dusty Knuckle – we brought back the Mackerel Pide for one day. We sold out more than 300 sandwiches within four hours. Queues of people yearning for a taste of the recent past blew us away. All proceeds went to the admirable charity Ahbap Platformu Resmi Sitesi (AHBAP), and a devastating natural disaster brought out the generous spirit of East London. The mackerel has always been a fortuitous creature for us – from the summer holidays of our youth, in Turkey, chomping away at mackerel sarnies by the Bosporus to years of having it on our menu at Mangal II as a grilled whole fish (my all-time favourite dish); from the Mackerel Pide to today's elevated and joyous iteration on our menu. Much to the delight of our customers, it will forever remain on our menu. If the little bit of safety and luck that it brought us during our most challenging times can be sprinkled to our homeland, all the better.

There is nothing more valuable than human life. Governments can delay lockdowns, resulting in thousands of needless deaths, and then overcompensate by enforcing the longest stretch of human confinement in modern, post-war history. And governments can allow poor infrastructure to be built because one crony is looking out for another. But the will of humanity persists, and the collective support is impregnable. Just ask the mackerel.

— Ferhat

Cooking

During its inception, the 'new' restaurant received mixed reactions from guests: it was deemed either brilliant or completely catastrophic. I was just focused on stopping the place from falling apart. We had given the restaurant a lick of paint and a shiny new grill, but that didn't fix the issue of the building being 1,000 years old. From the electricity to the staircase to the equipment, everything was difficult to manage. It wasn't like the new and shiny restaurants I was used to in Copenhagen; here, we had to do more with less. I was also developing my leadership style whilst learning how to run a business. I didn't arrive from Copenhagen equipped with these skills, so it was a run-before-you-walk situation.

I would often put a dish on the menu without trying it. Not to show off, but we physically didn't have time in the day. The menus were printed before the mise-en-place was ready and, by the time guests ordered a dish, we were compiling it for the first time to order. I'd frantically plate another dish whilst looking over to the front-of-house staff, asking *Do they like it? What don't they like? Are you sure it's good?* My poor staff. Their job is difficult enough as it is without me asking them to decipher the guests' facial expressions. Eventually, we found our rhythm (albeit unconventional). In fact, we came out with some real magic during that period.

I learnt to trust my instincts and to combine seasonal flavours in my head – and like working a muscle, it strengthened. I compiled entire menus without having tried the dishes (at one too many pop-ups, guilty!). It's an unusual way of working, but it worked for us – I took what I knew and memories of dishes or feelings, then imparted them onto food. The overall idea was that a dish couldn't be bad if the intention behind it was genuine. (Then again, I can recall a few questionable things we sold for real money.) Sure, it took a few tweaks, but we got there in the end.

Five months into opening, we had food critic Fay Maschler booked in. It was absolute chaos that day. I can't begin to describe the terror I felt – with our concept being reviewed so prematurely into my career as a head chef – but there we were. Everything had to be perfect;

every sauce was tasted; all the best meats were portioned and ready to go. The best desserts were set aside. At the time, she was no longer writing for the *London Evening Standard*, so we were stunned that she chose to dine here. Forty-five minutes into her meal, everything seemed to be going smoothly, when Ferhat exclaimed, 'Holy shit, that's Jay Rayner.' I retorted, 'Fuck off.' I looked across the road; his resemblance was uncanny. Surely not?

He walked towards the restaurant. 'I have a booking under ———— ————.' He sat down. We were being reviewed by two of the most influential critics in the UK, on the same Tuesday evening, at the same time. They didn't even acknowledge each other. Even guests were stunned; they didn't know what the fuck was going on. Some tables were making videos of them both and storying it on their Instagrams. It was the single most gut-wrenching service of our lives. We sent dish after dish after dish, trying to maintain our cool. We sent them both away, seemingly happy. I felt sick for weeks waiting for the reviews. Fay gave us a glowing mention in *Tatler* – that was one down. Jay's review was published the following Sunday in *The Guardian*, the most anticipated review of the week. I burst into tears when I read the title: 'It's brave and compelling and properly delicious.'

— Sertaç

Gilbert & George
and the Diriks

It is entirely rare for two individuals to eat out for dinner every single night for the past thirty years. For the very same two individuals to live together in a grand East London home without a kitchen. To dress the same. To walk in sync. To complete each other's sentences and pick up one another's mannerisms, so one ends and the other begins through one fluid motion. Synchronicity. For the same two gentlemen, born of different mothers – to emphasise, *not* twins – to work and create together, two minds working symbiotically as one genius artist. To be married to one another and yet never offer a public display of affection for decades. To be famous and wealthy but seek the humble delights of ocakbaşı cooking over fine-dining indulgences.

Gilbert and George, the renowned British artists, supported our father's cooking for over thirty years. Atheist men who devoutly abode their prophet wherever he laid his skewer: from my father's humble beginnings as a fiery young chef at 01 Adana in Newington Green in 1988, to his creation of Mangal I in 1990, to his eventual settlement at Mangal II in 1994. Gilbert and George (G&G) followed him every step of the way, every single night. Bar the odd Tuesday here and there when they'd dine at Dotori, the Japanese restaurant at Finsbury Park, because they had insider knowledge that the freshest sushi was being served that particular day. They'd return to Mangal II the following evening and sheepishly confess that – indeed, yes – they had visited their mistress the previous night and wanted to come clean.

Let's go back. Back to 1988. It is purely speculative to imagine what drew G&G to my father, but one can make an educated speculation. My father was finding his footing in his first few years in North London and formulating his plans to open the UK's first ever ocakbaşı whilst fine-tuning his craft over gas cookers. G&G would have stumbled upon an exciting young chef and felt something: a connection, desire and overwhelming dopamine hit in the man's cooking. They were about to commit to their dinner ritual, to dine at his restaurants nearly every night for three decades. After they'd already settled on the same caff for breakfast every day, now their evenings would be complete.

Why were they so rigid, so set on this dining routine? After all, if given the means, they could venture into a world of cuisines, establishments and experiences. Rarely would anybody return to the same place, night after night, year after year. I found it odd and eventually queried this with them. Their response? It's because they don't want to *think* about dinner. They don't want to expend their energy fretting and deliberating where to eat, how to book and who to have serve them. It frees up their brain space to focus on their art, their work, their life mission. They simply want automation in all aspects of life except the creative control they exert with their art. Which sounds a bit, well, resigned. Impersonal. Thankfully, George would add, 'We eat here every night out of love.' And the love was palpable. Their devotion to my father, his family, his staff and his establishment was very real and touching. They noticed minor changes with décor. They were very quick to spot a waiter's haircut. They'd be courteous and thankful at service. They'd make quips and share jokes with the team. They had their routine, but there was nothing robotic or distant with their demeanour once you were in their circle. Could they appear aloof to others? Yes. Even with their nearest and dearest, they had their off days and brought a small wall of protection where friendliness never crossed into over-familiarity. Occasionally, they'd step out of their comfort zones and attend Dirik family ceremonies, such as our sister's wedding, and my and Sertaç's rather embarrassing circumcision ceremony. (Known as *sünnet düğün,* this is a Bar Mitzvah of sorts for Turkish communities where everyone celebrates your penis.)

Sadly, all love must end, one way or another. My father stopped coming into work by the late 2010s. I grew up. I was a young man who possessed progressive, London-centric political and social ideals. Many restaurants rely on a connection between staff and patrons, and waitstaff must adapt their personalities oftentimes to complement the mood or personalities of a table. My father and some of our staff, at times, seemed to take on outdated subservient roles. But this wasn't for me. For better or worse, I was outspoken. I suspect my imprint on the restaurant brought an end to the romance. According to media outlets, the final straw came when I installed speakers in the restaurant so we could play music more in tune to my tastes as a Londoner.

When G&G eventually stopped coming in, I felt obliged to check if all was well after a few weeks. I rang their home, asked how they were doing and eventually confronted the elephant in the room. 'So, why have you both stopped coming in here every night?' The response was mildly pithy: They were now going to Mangal I, but they were sure to return to Mangal II soon one day, soon, maybe.

I felt some relief, to be honest. We changed the restaurant wholescale during COVID-19 and – honestly, my gut feeling is that they would they have hated this transformation. They seemed uncomfortable every time I acted confidently in my own restaurant. Now, my brother and I were thriving: we had acclaimed seasonal dishes, natural wines and English staff working for us.

Then, there's the other side of the coin. For all the development and growth with our establishment, we wouldn't have maintained our family business for thirty years without G&G. They were our main draw. Customers flocked to Mangal II to see them. We didn't pay for marketing; we didn't need to – two of the world's most celebrated living artists dined in our restaurant every night. We owe G&G a lot, as their loyal patronage kept us busy and ticking for decades. They championed us in every interview. They invited us to every exhibition. And the penis Bar Mitzvah thing – remember the sünnet düğün they attended? Truth is, they were extremely kind and polite towards us, to all of us who worked here. And to customers who'd approach them.

I'm a little saddened not to speak to them every evening. I even miss our soft debates. We were simply two opposite sides of the pole trying, yet failing, to meet in the middle. They found the conversations stimulating, hence their insistence on continuing them. I found them challenging, but it set me up to deal with people who didn't share my political ideals. Despite their beliefs, I still liked them as people. My dad adores them. And our family is eternally grateful for their existence: their art, their taste buds and their devotion. Every family has an estranged, weird uncle. We have two, conjoined as one entity.

— Ferhat

Smoked Olive Oil

This smoked olive oil appears in many of the dishes within these pages. It is essential to exercise caution when preparing the oil. You must work outdoors and away from flammable materials. Once you combine the two ingredients, it will flare up. I recommend reading the recipes a couple times so you can come prepared and work confidently.

Makes 500 ml (17 fl oz/
     generous 2 cups)

500 ml (17 fl oz/generous 2 cups)
     olive oil
1 smouldering charcoal

Working outdoors in an open space, place the olive oil in a metal container (or a cast-iron pot) with a lid. Using tongs, very carefully lower the smouldering charcoal into the oil. It will flare up and begin to smoke, so you should act quickly by covering it with a lid. Step back at least 1 metre/yard away when this happens.

Set aside for an hour to infuse. Strain through a fine-mesh sieve.

Left-over oil can be stored in an airtight container.

Cultured Kaymak and Cultured Butter

Traditionally, Turkish yogurt is made with buffalo milk, whereby the fattiest layer sets on top – that's *kaymak*, the crème de la crème of yogurt. We make ours with double (heavy) cream and introduce an active yogurt culture, then ferment it near the grill for three days. (We keep the kaymak on a shelf located under the grill.)

Makes 1 kg (34 oz/4¼ cups)

1 kg (34 oz/4¼ cups) double
   (heavy) cream
20 g/¾ oz live yogurt

Cultured kaymak Heat the double (heavy) cream in a large pan over medium-low heat until it reaches a temperature of 40°C/104°F. Remove the pan from the heat. Stir in the live yogurt, then pour the mixture into a sterilised non-metallic container. Place a clean dish cloth over the container and seal it with an elastic band. You want the dairy to breathe.

Leave it somewhere warm to ferment, stirring once a day, for 3 days or until it's reached the desired level of sourness. (It should taste like crème fraîche.) Refrigerate for 24 hours.

Cultured butter Place the kaymak into a mixer or food processor. Add 2 ice cubes and blend until the cream splits. If it hasn't split, continue to add 2 more at time. Pour the mixture into a clean, dry towel and squeeze out all the buttermilk. Set aside.

Roll the butter into balls and wrap in clingfilm (plastic wrap). It can be stored in the refrigerator for up to a week.

Mangal II Pickles

Makes 1 kg/2 lbs 4 oz

2 L (68 fl oz/8½ cups) white vinegar
350 g (12 oz/1¾ cups) sugar
4 tablespoons fine salt
2 teaspoons black peppercorns
2 teaspoons coriander seeds
1½ teaspoons sumac
1 teaspoon black (urfa) chilli flakes
1 kg/2 lbs 4 oz vegetables, such as
    chillies, onions, carrots, radishes,
    turnips, beetroots (beets) or
    cucumbers, cut into desired shape

Combine all the ingredients except the vegetables in a large pan. Pour in 1.2 L (40 fl oz/5 cups) of water, then bring to a boil. Strain into a large sterilised glass jar.

Add the vegetables, then set aside to cool. Place a J-cloth over top to submerge the vegetables. Cover, then refrigerate overnight.

Left-over pickles can be stored in an airtight container in the refrigerator for up to a month.

Grilled Chickpea Hummus

Serves 6

500 g (1 lb 2 oz/2 ¼ cups) dried
   chickpeas, soaked overnight
4 teaspoons sunflower oil
80 ml (3 oz/⅓ cup) tahini
1½ tablespoons lemon juice
1 clove garlic, minced
1½ teaspoons salt
1¼ teaspoons white pepper
2 teaspoons garlic powder
Smoked Olive Oil (page 100),
   for drizzling
Store-bought or home-made Pide
   (page 120), to serve (optional)

Drain the chickpeas. Place in a large pan and add twice its volume in cold water. Bring to a boil, then simmer for 45 minutes. Drain well, then set aside in a colander to drain for another hour.

Preheat a charcoal grill over high heat until the coals are white hot. Oil half of the chickpeas. Add the oiled chickpeas to a grill sieve (or metal sieve) and grill for 5 minutes, until charred all over. (If using a metal sieve, toss continuously.)

Transfer both charred and cooked chickpeas to a blender and pulse until broken down. Add the remaining ingredients and blend until smooth. If grainy, add 1 or 2 ice cubes.

Drizzle with smoked olive oil and serve with pide, if using.

Smoked Oil Tarama

Tarama is simply the Turkish word for taramasalata. Bright pink, courtesy of beetroot (beet) juice, our more rustic version is often found in *meyhanes*, a type of traditional Turkish restaurant. We've added smoke to lean into our namesake.

Serves 4–6

750 g/1 lb 10 oz smoked cod's roe
300 ml (10 fl oz/1¼ cups) milk
4 slices white bread, crusts removed
20 cloves garlic
2½ tablespoons lemon juice
300 ml (10 fl oz/1¼ cups) Smoked
    Olive Oil (page 100), plus extra
    for drizzling
Salt, to taste
Aleppo chilli flakes, for sprinkling
Store-bought or home-made Pide
    (page 120), to serve

Peel the skins off the smoked cod's roe. (They can be frozen and later added to sauces and infusions.)

Pour the milk into a shallow bowl. Dip the bread into the milk for 5–10 seconds. Do not saturate the bread as we need some texture to aid the overall consistency. Transfer the bread to a blender, then add the roe, garlic and lemon juice. Purée until smooth. With the motor still running, slowly pour in the smoked olive oil and blend until emulsified. The roe adds enough saltiness but season with more salt, if needed.

Place a mound of purée on a plate. Using a spoon, create a well in the centre. Fill with smoked olive oil, then sprinkle with chilli flakes. Serve with pide.

Cured Bass
with Çoban Water

Çoban salata, or Shepherd's Salad (page 60), is a traditional
Turkish salad prepared with tomatoes and cucumbers.
Here, its flavours are used to season cured sea bass fillets.

Serves 4

200 g/7 oz skinless sea bass fillets,
    pinbones removed
2½ teaspoons fine salt
½ teaspoon sugar
4 tomatoes
2 cucumbers
½ onion
Juice of 1 lemon
Aleppo chilli flakes, for sprinkling

Place the fillets on a plate and season all over with ½ teaspoon
of salt and the sugar. Refrigerate, uncovered, for 1 hour to cure.

Combine the tomatoes, cucumbers, onion, lemon juice and 2 teaspoons of salt in a food processor and process until smooth. Pour
the mixture into a container and freeze for 2 hours, until frozen.

Line a fine-mesh sieve with muslin (cheesecloth) and set over
a bowl. Place the frozen mixture into the sieve and set aside in
the refrigerator to defrost. The liquid should be clarified once
it's strained.

Finely slice the sea bass. Pour over the çoban water, then sprinkle
the Aleppo chilli flakes on top. Serve cold.

Okra with
Sucuk Jam

Serves 4

150 g (5¼ oz/¾ cup) sugar
5 tablespoons honey
2 teaspoons ground cinnamon
300 g/10½ oz Sucuk (page 200),
    casing removed
4 dried smoked chillies such as ancho
1 teaspoon green cardamom pods
1½ tablespoons sunflower oil,
    for frying
300 g/10½ oz okra, cleaned and
    halved lengthwise
2 teaspoons lemon juice

In a small pan, combine the sugar, honey and cinnamon. Add 3½ tablespoons of water and heat over medium heat, until the sugar has dissolved.

Break up sucuk into small pieces, then add it to the pan. Sauté for 15 minutes, until browned. Stir in the chillies and cardamom and cook for another 5 minutes. Discard 2 chillies. Transfer the mixture to a blender and blend until smooth.

Heat the oil in a large frying pan over very high heat. Add the okra and fry for 3 minutes, until seared on all sides.

Plate the sucuk jam. Top with the okra, squeeze over some lemon juice and serve immediately.

Courgette Fritters
with Sucuk Mayonnaise

Serves 4

For the courgette fritters
4 carrots, coarsely grated
2 large potatoes, coarsely grated
1 courgette (zucchini),
    coarsely grated
1 tablespoon salt
30 g (1 oz/½ cup) finely chopped dill
2 tablespoons finely chopped parsley
50 g (1¾ oz/⅓ cup) plain
    (all-purpose) flour
2½ tablespoons potato starch
2 eggs, beaten

For the sucuk mayonnaise
100 g/3½ oz store-bought or
    home-made Sucuk (page 200)
500 ml (17 fl oz/generous 2 cups)
    sunflower oil
4 egg yolks
Salt, to taste
Lemon juice, to taste

Assembly
Sunflower oil, for frying
Lemon wedges, to serve

Courgette fritters In a large bowl, combine the carrots, potatoes, courgettes (zucchini) and salt. Set aside for 30–45 minutes.

Transfer the mixture into a clean dish towel, then squeeze out the moisture until it is relatively dry. Stir in the dill and parsley.

Sift the flour and potato starch into the mixture, then add the eggs. Combine until the mixture is sticky and homogenous. Set aside.

Sucuk mayonnaise Heat a large frying pan over medium-high heat. Add the sucuk and break it up using a wooden spoon. Pour in the oil and cook for 10 minutes, until the oil is orange-red and aromatic. Set aside to cool.

Transfer the sucuk and oil into a blender and pulse until the sucuk is completely broken down. Set aside for 3 hours to infuse, then strain and refrigerate the oil.

In a blender, combine the egg yolks and oil and blend until emulsified. Season with salt and/or lemon juice.

Assembly Heat the oil in a frying pan over medium heat. Working in batches to avoid overcrowding, scoop heaped tablespoons of batter into the pan. Using a spatula, flatten the fritters and pan-fry for a minute on each side, until caramelized. Transfer to a paper towel–lined plate to drain.

Serve hot with the sucuk mayonnaise and lemon wedges.

Three-Bean Stew

This is one of my favourite dishes to prepare during late summer when samphire is in season and tomatoes and beans are the freshest.

Serves 4

200 g/7 oz fresh white beans such
    as coco beans
200 g/7 oz fresh borlotti beans
Fine salt, plus extra to season
100 g/3½ oz samphire
2 tablespoons olive oil, plus extra
    for brushing
200 g/7 oz green beans, trimmed
2 vine-ripened tomatoes
1 small onion, finely chopped
6 cloves garlic, minced
2 teaspoons tomato purée (paste)
100 ml (3½ fl oz/scant ½ cup)
    chicken stock
Lemon rind
Black pepper

To serve
White rice
Pickles
Pickled chillies
Thinly sliced onions

Preheat a charcoal grill over high heat until the coals are white hot.

In a medium pan, combine the fresh beans, 2 teaspoons of salt and enough cold water to cover. Bring to a boil, then reduce the heat to medium-low and simmer for 30 minutes. Drain.

Bring a small pan of water to a boil. Fill a bowl with iced water. Add the samphire to the boiling water and blanch for 3 minutes. Using tongs, transfer the samphire to the ice bath to shock. Pat dry with paper towels, then put into a bowl and drizzle with 1 tablespoon of olive oil.

Slice the green beans into two segments. Place them in a grill basket and brush with oil. Grill for 3–4 minutes, until charred on both sides. Set aside.

Set a cast-iron grate onto the grill and heat up. Brush the tomatoes with oil, then grill for 5 minutes, until thoroughly charred on all sides. Transfer the tomatoes to a food processor or blender and pulse until broken down.

Heat the remaining tablespoon of oil in a frying pan over medium heat. Add the onions and garlic and sauté for 3 minutes, until the onions are caramelized. Add the tomato purée (paste) and cook for another minute. Stir in the grilled tomatoes and stock and simmer until the mixture has reduced by half. Add all the beans and lemon rind and simmer for 10 minutes. Season with pepper.

Transfer to a serving bowl and garnish with samphire. Serve immediately with white rice, pickles, chillies and onions.

Bread

A restaurant needs their own bread. We used to buy in seventy-five loaves of long Turkish pide from a local bakery, par-cooked so they could be finished on the grill. These delicious, freshly made yeasted breads were ideal for soaking up juices under mixed kebab platters or for dipping warm into perfectly whipped (and pink) mass-produced taramasalata. Unfortunately, they didn't work with our new dishes.

We had to make our own bread – no matter if I changed the menu, suppliers or kitchen set-up. There's no point of making declarations about our food philosophy or evolution if we don't make the only symbolic food item that encapsulates a restaurant in a single bite... bread. There was just one problem: I didn't know how to bake.

But I was also lucky. I had an adept, agile and hard-working team who stood by me during those early months and would become a part of something special. This incredible crew helped the restaurant take form: Arthur Bonham Carter, Leyla Göktepe, Zak Rowley and Nasuf Serifi.

We trialled, tested and failed... and failed... and failed. We used a sourdough starter by Arthur's dad and soon learnt of breadmaking's complexities. I was obsessed. We treated that dough like a newborn child – searching for a room in which it was happiest, establishing the frequency of feedings and determining its favoured water temperature. For five months, we bent every which direction to adjust the recipe over and over again. We tried baking our breads in the most basic of convection ovens, one which indicated the incorrect temperature on its screen and had no steaming capabilities (yet we still use it to this day). We even tried to fry the dough, which resulted in something that resembled a *pizza fritti* – tasty but not Turkish.

Eventually, we placed a cast-iron grate on the mangal. We dipped the dough into olive oil, hand-pulled it into a disk and laid it carefully over ripping coals. Then, something magical happened. It rose. It charred. It was alive. At last, we had beautiful grilled breads with airy pockets and little charred blisters. It was gently sour yet earthy, laced with an electric, smoky undercurrent.

Our Grilled Sourdough Pide (page 120) is undeniably Mangal II. It represents the flavour profile and energy of our restaurant. Everyone tasted a piece; eyes rolled back; we all smiled. Finally, we had done it.

We are a family of butchers and grillers with collective generational knowledge. For more than two decades, we were famed for our variety of grilled meats. The bread was always a little treat at the end, perhaps a side note, to the platters of fantastic meats we piled high. It has gone from filler to killer. Today, it steals the show.

— Sertaç

Grilled Sourdough Pide

We feed our starter every morning. The yeast is fully developed when it smells sour and bubbles and has doubled in size. Another good indication of a readied yeast is that it will float when added to water. Give it a good mix and pour it into the flour mixture.

Makes 20 (70-g/2½-oz) rolls

For the pre-ferment
50 g (1¾ oz/⅓ cup) strong
   bread flour
50 g (1¾ oz/⅓ cup) wholemeal
   (whole wheat) flour
100 ml (3½ fl oz/scant ½ cup) water
6 g/⅛ oz sourdough leaven

For the sourdough pide
640 g (1 lb 6 oz/5½ cups) strong
   bread flour, plus extra for dusting
160 g (5½ oz/1 cup) wholemeal flour
1¼ tablespoons salt
Olive oil, for coating and dipping
Smoked Olive Oil (page 100),
   for sprinkling
Sea salt, for sprinkling
Butter or your favourite toppings,
   to serve

Pre-ferment Combine all the ingredients and mix well. Set aside somewhere warm for 2–3 hours, until sour, bubbly and doubled in size. Makes 200 g/7 oz.

Sourdough pide In a large container or the bowl of a stand mixer fitted with a hook attachment, combine the flours. ❶❷ Add 520 ml (17½ fl oz/2¼ cups) of water and 200 g/7 oz of pre-ferment. ❸ Mix with your hands for 15 minutes or on low speed for 3 minutes, until it comes together. ❹ Set aside for 30 minutes to develop the yeast.

In a small bowl, combine the salt and 2½ tablespoons of warm water. Add it to the dough, then knead by hand for 15 minutes or mix for 5 minutes. ❺❻ Place the dough into a large bowl that's double its size. Rub a light coating of olive oil on top and cover with a dish towel. ❼❽❾ Set aside somewhere warm for 45 minutes.

Coil fold the dough by freeing up the sides of the dough in the bowl. To do this, grab the centre of the dough and pull it up, allowing both ends to fall into the centre whilst simultaneously rotating it 90 degrees. Give it two turns. This technique forces air into the dough and builds tension. Rest for 30 minutes. Repeat three more times. Rest the dough in the refrigerator for 1 hour.

Place the dough on a clean work counter lightly dusted with flour. Weigh out 70-g/2½-oz pieces and roll them into balls. (Wearing powder-free latex gloves with a little bit of olive oil makes it easier to work with the sticky dough.) Cup the dough and turn it in quick circular motions against the work counter to guarantee tension and ensure you have a smooth ball. Place the balls on a baking sheet and cover with a clean dish towel. Set aside to prove (proof) for 1 hour, until doubled in size.

⌐

Meanwhile, preheat a charcoal grill over high heat until the coals are white hot. Lay down a cast-iron grill grate. To ensure you have continuous, even heat from the coals throughout the grilling process, wave your hand over different areas of the grate to determine the hot spots. If it's uneven, spread the coals and wait a minute for the heat to disperse.

Dip the dough into a bowl of olive oil. Without pushing out too much air, carefully hand-stretch the dough to a 15-cm/6-inch diameter. I leave a 1-cm/½-inch border around the edge where I want my bubbles to sit. Carefully lay the dough down, retaining as much of the disk shape as possible. (The shape of when it was laid down will be the set shape when grilling.) Place the pide on the grill and grill for a minute, until cooked on one side. Using tongs, flip the pide and grill for another 30 seconds–1 minute. Set aside to cool. Repeat with the remaining pides. Avoid stacking the grilled pides, which releases their air.

Sprinkle a few drops of smoked olive oil and a little sea salt on top. Serve immediately on its own with some butter or add your favourite toppings.

Mackerel Pide

Store-bought mackerel fillets tend to be v-cut, meaning that the bones are trimmed along the spine to give it a 'v' shape. If you're buying them whole, you can ask your fishmonger to do this or simply remove the pinbones yourself.

Serves 4

For the mackerel pide
4 mackerel fillets, pinbones removed

For the dill oil
1 bunch dill
½ bunch parsley
4 teaspoons salt, plus extra to taste
500 ml (17 fl oz/generous 2 cups)
    sunflower oil
4 egg yolks, cold
4 teaspoons lemon juice

Assembly
1 store-bought or home-made Pide
    (page 120) or large focaccia
Smoked Olive Oil (page 100),
    for drizzling
1½ tablespoons black (urfa)
    chilli flakes

Mackerel pide Dry the mackerel, uncovered, in the refrigerator for 24 hours.

Dill oil Combine the dill, parsley, salt and oil in a blender and blend until the mixture is smooth and vibrant green. Cover and refrigerate for 2 hours to steep.

Line a fine-mesh sieve with muslin (cheesecloth) and place it over a plastic bowl. Pour in the mixture and leave it to strain. Freeze for 30 minutes.

In a blender, combine the dill oil and egg yolks. Working with cold ingredients prevents the oil from splitting. (However, if it does split, add a very small amount of iced water.) Add the lemon juice and season with salt. Refrigerate until needed.

Assembly Heat a charcoal grill over medium heat. Place a stainless-steel grill rack directly over the coals.

When hot, add the mackerel, skin-side down. Give the grate a tap every 10–20 seconds to prevent the mackerel from sticking to it. Grill for 5 minutes, until the skin has caramelized. Transfer the mackerel to a plate and set aside for 2 minutes to cook in the residual heat.

Meanwhile, slice the pide into two disks. Toast for 2 minutes on the hot grill. Place the bottom half of the pide on a plate, then spread out the emulsion. Top with the mackerel, then add the remaining half. Drizzle with the smoked olive oil and sprinkle with black (urfa) chilli flakes.

Lamb Heart Pide

Serves 4

2 teaspoons salt, plus extra to taste
1 teaspoon sugar
3 cloves garlic
½ onion
Peel of 1 lemon
1 bay leaf
1 teaspoon sweet pepper flakes
    (tatlı pul biber)
1 lamb heart
300 ml (10 fl oz/1¼ cups) sunflower
    oil, plus extra for brushing
2½ tablespoons ground cumin,
    plus extra for sprinkling
1½ tablespoons dried oregano
1 egg yolk
4 teaspoons lemon juice
1 pickled cucumber (page 158),
    finely chopped
4 store-bought or home-made Pide
    (page 120), to serve

In a large bowl, combine salt, sugar, 250 ml (8 fl oz/1 cup) of water and 250 g/9 oz ice. Using an immersion blender, mix until completely dissolved. (This allows you to see the clarity of your brine, which will become clear again once the salt and sugar are dissolved.) Add the garlic, onion, lemon peel, bay leaf and sweet pepper flakes (tatlı pul biber).

Split the lamb heart into half, removing the arteries and the webbing (valves). Add the lamb heart to the brine and brine overnight or for 12 hours.

Preheat a charcoal grill over high heat until the coals are white hot.

Remove the lamb heart from the brine and skewer. Refrigerate to set.

Meanwhile, in a blender, combine the oil, oregano and cumin. Pour into a pitcher (jug) and refrigerate for 1 hour.

In a blender, combine the egg yolk, lemon juice and 4 teaspoons of water. Blend. Slowly pour in the chilled seasoned oil and blend until emulsified. Season with salt. Fold in the pickled cucumber.

Brush the lamb heart with oil. Add the lamb heart to the grill and grill for 2½ minutes on each side, until seared. Set aside to rest for 3–5 minutes.

Add the cucumber mixture to a freshly grilled pide. Slice the lamb heart and arrange on top. Finish with a sprinkling of cumin and serve hot.

Grilled Octopus
with Butter Beans

Serves 4–6

500 g (1 lb 2 oz/2¾ cups) dried
    butter (lima) beans
1 teaspoon bicarbonate of soda
    (baking soda)
300 g/10½ oz whole octopus,
    beak removed
2 tablespoons olive oil, plus extra
    for drizzling
1 small onion, chopped
10 cloves garlic, finely chopped
2½ teaspoons dried oregano
1 teaspoon Aleppo chilli flakes
1 teaspoon paprika
4–5 tomatoes, coarsely grated
3½ tablespoons Smoked Olive Oil
    (page 100)
Sunflower oil, for brushing
Chopped parsley, for garnish
    (optional)

Put the butter (lima) beans and bicarbonate of soda (baking soda) into a bowl. Add enough water to cover, then soak overnight.

Drain the beans. Place them in a pan, then add enough cold water to cover. Bring to a boil, then cook for 10 minutes. Reduce the heat to medium-low, cover and simmer for 45 minutes, until the beans are softened but not broken. Drain well, then chill.

Meanwhile, bring a stockpot of salted water to a boil. Add the octopus and simmer for 30 minutes, until cooked through. Set aside to cool. Using tongs, transfer the octopus to a bowl, then drizzle it with the olive oil. Refrigerate for 1 hour.

Heat 2 tablespoons of olive oil in a large frying pan over high heat. Add the onions, garlic, oregano, chilli flakes and paprika and sauté for 4 minutes, until the onion starts to caramelize. Stir in the tomato and smoked olive oil and cook for another 15 minutes, until reduced. Add the butter beans.

Separate the tentacles and head. Discard the head. Slice the tentacles into 2.5-cm/1-inch pieces. Skewer the pieces, then brush them with the sunflower oil. Place them on the grill and grill for 3–4 minutes, until charred all over.

Plate the octopus and butter beans. Garnish with parsley, if using, and serve.

Grilled Chicken Thighs

Serves 6

2 tablespoons black peppercorns
4 teaspoons ground cumin
2½ teaspoons dried oregano
2 teaspoons Aleppo chilli flakes
250 g (9 oz/1½ cups) salt
6 tablespoons sugar
4 L (135 fl oz/17 cups) buttermilk
3 tablespoons Turkish tomato
    paste (*domates salçası*) or tomato
    purée (paste)
12 boneless, skin-on chicken thighs

To serve (optional)
Fresh vegetables
Grilled vegetables
Rice
Mangal II Pickles (page 104)
Sumac onions
Lemon wedge

In a small bowl, combine the pepper, cumin, oregano and chilli flakes. Mix well.

In a separate bowl, combine the salt, sugar and 1 L (34 fl oz/ 4¼ cups) of cold water. Using an immersion blender or spoon, mix until completely dissolved. Stir in the buttermilk, tomato paste and spice blend. Add the chicken thighs, then marinate overnight.

Preheat a charcoal grill over medium heat until the coals are white hot. Shake off the excess liquid from the chicken, then skewer the thighs. Place the skewers on the hot grill and grill the chicken for 5 minutes on each side, until cooked through.

Serve with vegetables, rice, pickles, sumac onions and a lemon wedge, if desired.

TFC (Turkish Fried Chicken Livers)

Offal is championed in Turkey – it can be pan-fried, grilled, sautéed or stewed. In this recipe, we brine it in buttermilk, then deep-fry it. You want to use a good amount of flour to create the textured crumb.

Serves 6

For the chicken livers
1 tablespoon black pepper
1 teaspoon Aleppo chilli flakes
2½ teaspoons dried oregano
2 teaspoons ground cumin
4 tablespoons salt
3 tablespoons sugar
2 L (68 fl oz/8½ cups) buttermilk
1 kg/2 lbs 4 oz chicken livers
2 L (68 fl oz/8½ cups) sunflower oil,
    for frying
Lemon wedges, to serve

For the seasoned flour
1 kg (2 lbs 4 oz/7 cups) plain
    (all-purpose) flour
200 g (7 oz/1¾ cups) cornflour
    (cornstarch)
4 tablespoons dried oregano
2 tablespoons paprika
2 tablespoons ground cumin
1½ tablespoons sweet pepper
    flakes (tatlı pul biber)
1½ tablespoons salt
1½ tablespoons black pepper

Chicken livers In a small bowl, combine the black pepper, chilli flakes, oregano and cumin. Mix well.

In a separate bowl, combine the salt, sugar and 500 ml (17 fl oz/generous 2 cups) of water. Using an immersion blender, mix until completely dissolved. (This allows you to see the clarity of your brine, which will become clear again once the salt and sugar are dissolved.) Stir in the buttermilk and spice blend. Add the chicken livers and marinate covered in the refrigerator overnight.

Seasoned flour Combine all the ingredients in a large bowl.

Heat the oil in a deep fryer or deep pan to 160°C/325°F. Transfer the liver pieces into the seasoned flour, ensuring they are fully coated. Do not shake off the excess batter or flour, both of which help to create the needed texture.

Working in batches to avoid overcrowding, carefully lower 3–4 chicken livers into the hot oil. Fry for 3–4 minutes, until cooked through and golden on both sides. Transfer the livers to a wire rack to drain. Repeat with the remaining livers.

Place the fried chicken livers on a serving platter and serve immediately with lemon wedges.

Douglas Pine Künefe

Künefe, or *knafeh*, is a traditional Turkish dessert made with kadayif pastry, cheese and a lemon syrup. Here, to celebrate citrus season, we've used pink navel oranges (Cara Cara) and Douglas pine, a type of fir that tastes like grapefruit. The rind of a grapefruit can be used in place of pine.

Serves 4

500 g (1 lb 2 oz/2½ cups) sugar
1 teaspoon citric acid
100 g/3½ oz Douglas pine needles
400 g/12 oz kadayif pastry
300 g (10½ oz/2⅔ cups) processed
    mozzarella, coarsely grated
300 g/10½ oz brown or
    melted butter
Cultured Kaymak (page 102),
    to serve
1 orange, segmented, to serve

In a pan, combine the sugar, citric acid and 500 ml (17 fl oz/generous 2 cups) of water. Bring to a boil, then add the pine needles. Set aside for 1 hour to infuse, then refrigerate for 24 hours.

Strain the syrup through a fine-mesh sieve.

Place a layer of the kadayif pastry into a künefe tray (or frying pan). Add the mozzarella, then cover with more pastry.

Preheat a charcoal grill over high heat until the coals are white hot. Set a cast-iron grate on top. Put the künefe tray on the grill, drizzle the pastry with butter and cook until the bottom of the pastry begins to caramelize. Flip over and grill for 5 minutes, until caramelized on both sides.

Remove the pan from the grill and immediately ladle over the syrup. Soak for 2–3 minutes.

Serve hot with a spoon of cultured kaymak and orange slices.

INSPIRATION

Recipes Influenced by
Family and Heritage

When you're adapting a restaurant as old as ours, it's important to tread carefully. In our case, there was a written formula that was older than I was, with customers who had dined there for decades. It was imperative that we respected the rules that kept us afloat for more than twenty-five years.

In Turkey, this is known as *vijdan*, meaning 'conscience'. It's embedded in our culture to approach everything with care, particularly when it refers to people or practices older than yourself. The ethos was simple: we could prepare the most delicious dish in the world, but if we couldn't find a Turkish point of reference, then it wasn't a dish for Mangal II. The dishes didn't have to look like the traditional Turkish food everyone expects to see, but the nuances of flavour, smell and texture would all be there. The building itself still welcomes you with warmth, a slight waft of smoke and the sizzle of meat rendering over the grill. Treading this line carefully sounds limiting but, in truth, it forces ideas that would otherwise never be discovered to come to light.

Reading and conversing about age-old practices, finding the best local produce to emulate those authentic Turkish flavours and making the connections to serve within our setting... this was our formula. The rules are fundamental if you plan on breaking them.

— Sertaç

Recipes

Mum

Bless our mum. When I think back to my childhood, I remember her as someone who would never sit still. She was working on something constantly: fixing up the house, cleaning, knitting or painting. But, more often than not, she was cooking.

Turks are so incredibly food centric. I would hover around her in the kitchen, and she would have me try the dishes in all their cooking stages, from raw vegetables to parcooked to perfectly stewed. I would help her wrap sarma, fill manti and make stews and rice. In Turkish culture, I was regarded as the perfect child – not because I was well-mannered, but because I was fat.

In the winter, she'd preserve our garden vegetables in the most delicious, garlicky, spicy brine and serve the pickles in the early spring alongside tender, slow-cooked lamb that practically disintegrated amongst the vegetables. She'd dry her own fruit liquids and transform them into fruit leathers. We were spoiled by the environment my parents created for us in Chingford – they weren't setting it up to be hip or cool; rather, they wanted to create a life worth remembering in a country that bore little resemblance to their homeland. Here was her patch of land where she could retain her values.

Though the restaurant's identity is deeply rooted in Turkish grill culture, I wanted to show the spectrum of Turkish cuisine. My cooking has been heavily influenced by my mum's food and my upbringing. My dishes are often the ones she used to show me, enhanced with a grill or smoke element to make them relevant to the restaurant. We have variations of sarmas (page 168), manti (page 163), böreks (page 154) and künefe (page 134). These are all of my mum's dishes.

My dad's cooking style is so deeply rooted into the restaurant. The introduction of our mum's style made the restaurant feel whole for me. And with it came a newfound respect for Turkish cuisine – restaurant guests pivoted their needs for meat on rice and kept arriving for the new dishes. We changed people's eating habits; the remarks went from 'I'll have my usual' to 'What's new on the menu?'

— Sertaç

Cull Yaw: A Voyage to the World's Greatest Sheep

For a family raised on lamb – fed it for breakfast, lunch and dinner by a father who regards sheep as something to inhale like air – it made sense for me and Sertaç to level up and make the pilgrimage to the home of the world's best-tasting mutton. Discovering the Cornwall Project, we receive an invitation after sliding in a few DMs, a little to-and-fro and a shameless campaign of flattery.

It's stupid o'clock. We travel from East London to Paddington. We board the train after working the previous night's late shift and try to have a little shut eye, but we are too wired with excitement to drift off. We spend the entire journey pondering with mesmeric fascination what could be in store for us. We disembark in Exeter in Devon. We're off to meet the man himself, Matt Chatfield, and expect a Cornish experience of seagulls, azure blue seas, coastal breezes and life-affirming pastures. That's not to say Devon doesn't have that; it probably does. But when your man pulls up in his mum's old estate car, you think: Basque country, Patagonia, Kobe City this is not.

In Japan, the champion eponymously named cattle raised in the Hyogo prefecture lay in a vision of Studio Ghibli utopia, with clouds touching hill tops, the greenest of grassland and the most imposing cows giving you the dead-eye stare. On the contrary, the cull yaw here are a different breed altogether – literally, obviously, but also in how these most flavoursome sheep are not reared in a Sound of Music-esque landscape.

When we meet, we exchange warm greetings and sit in the car with the radio static and frequency fluctuating more than a turbulent teenage relationship. We accept that it's going to be one hell of a day. He is talkative, Matt, and can charm the wool off a spring lamb. Conversation starts rapidly, excitedly, as if we're old uni flatmates having a catch up after many years. Affable, giddy and full of interesting thoughts, Matt immediately puts us at ease. The vibe is set to instant (God, I hate this word) banter. We drive for an hour and discover that a) we love lamb and sheep as something to devour but also as an animal to cherish and b) we hate the same people – well, for the most part anyway. United by love and hate. The day only gets better and better.

We drive past lots of muddy one-way country roads and hand-written signs for farm entrances, whilst the endless grey clouds bring tension in the humidity. The funny-looking sheep scatter around. We finally arrive at the digs. First sight: a huge barn with no visible gate. Stashed inside are Matt's belongings, just out in the open for any thief to steal. His house is being rebuilt and, for now, this is home, a period of transition. It seems apt. Matt is in rural England, exposed, with nothing but green fields all around as his flock surround him, blanket him and envelop his family's land. Matt and the flock: it has a nice ring to it. I envy the man. He is removed from council tax, noisy neighbours, road works, Costa Coffee, ugly new builds, littering, loud motorbikes and bus diversions. He is surrounded by beautiful creatures, untainted forests, verdant landscapes, the smell of earth, the light of the stars, the absence of man in any vicinity and the sound of 'baaaas'.

He explains what he does, how he came to do it, the challenges he faces and his aspirations for regenerative farming. Admittedly, this world is not my forte and I am criminally ignorant to it all, but the experience is an education and I ascertain a few things.

Chemical fertilisers are bad. They destroy the soil and all the natural habitats and insects in the ecosystem beneath our feet. The most conventional livestock farming uses this toxic practice to ensure optimal output. It fucks up the environment, and the meat is tainted. Matt watched a lot of YouTube videos when he was working in hospitality in London. He also partied and had his fair deal of psychedelic moments, perhaps helping him tap into a deeper consciousness of his roots and his mother's farmland on the Cornwall-Devon border. He returned home with a mission.

His calling? He wanted to farm sheep, not lamb. He purchased lamb from the auction and, instead of raising them for a few paltry months, he nurtured them to old age. Though he was fond of his flock and attached to the sheep who displayed the most character and wit (he refused to cull any of his favourites, because it left him feeling shit), this symbiotic relationship with the sheep was more than goodwill.

The land he inherited from his mother was chemically fertilised. With an understanding of regenerative farming, he only purchased de-wormed lamb that grazed the land by eating the centre of the reeds. (Grassland didn't exist, because fertilisation had damaged the soil.) The sheep excrement would be consumed by dung beetles and worms, thereby loosening up and aerating the damaged soil and adding nutrients. Grass eventually grew.

As the sheep work to graze the ground, one patch at a time, the healed land turns green. The aim is to transform the soil, and the neighbouring woodland leased from his uncle, into a beautiful, healthy, biodiverse ecosystem.

We meet the team, and sure enough some sheep are friendlier than others. They're old, right? Some of the grumpier, more hostile

sheep almost charge at us, like a bull to a matador, and all I can think is, I hope you get culled. My caveperson instincts take over, and it comforts me to think the naughtier ones will be consumed at Mangal II soon. But the cute purr up next to us, like housecats seeking affection. I stroke the beasts, with pangs of guilt over my relentless consumption of its kind for more than three decades.

And why go through this bother? Because we, as a business, as a partnership between brothers, champion the best produce. We want to flip the script of our own lamb-centric backstory and improve the way we deliver the tastiest meat. The ethically farmed, long-living and nurtured mutton makes these pursuits worthwhile, highlighting them and, ultimately, serving them to the delight of the public.

We walk, talk and see the flock in action, grazing away the parts of land they've cultivated and the parts they have yet to. It leaves us in awe to see the proof of the work and the malleability of a land receptive to recovery. It is remarkable how forgiving it is and how quick it is to atone the sins of its past and move forward with positivity. We enter a woodland that Matt claims has been uninhabited for as long as he remembers. It is all untamed forest and streams and darkness and mystique. He will slowly veer his flock in this direction to cultivate the vast land, too, one bit at a time.

We see the lack of human imprint here: there are no traces of rubbish, wood carvings, chopped branches or footmarks. It feels surreal, being somewhere so removed from the toxic brutality of man. We venture deep into the woods, forging a path and piss-taking along the way. We're like scouts on a wild mission, and the inner child is on a fun adventure. As we make the loop around, I spot a huge pair of horns in the distance.

I stop Matt and Sertaç, gesture them to be silent and point to what's ahead: a giant stag. The huge bastard was stalking us. They see it, and Matt confirms my worst fears: the angry big boy is incensed that we're on his turf. He wants to drive us out, which is fair, absolutely fair. We have no right being there in the first place. We respect him as much as we want to run away from him. Boy, do we run. We run and run all the way. We enter a tunnel (Lord knows when it was built) and run through its shallow passage in the river, getting our feet soaked as we try to escape the threat of being mauled by a woodland beast. I'd love to think we outwitted the stag but, truth is, it probably took one look at us and realised – with all the cigarettes, alcohol and crap between us – our bodies weren't worth the effort.

Back to open land, it's time to call it a day. I'm starving by this point, and I presume cull yaw isn't on the menu. We head to Philip Warren Butchers, who buy up all of Matt's ewe and convert it into delicious meats. We visit the cold rooms where they're aged, and it's a sight to behold. Racks of mutton, beef and pork, all cut into delectable shapes and sizes, are hanging, drying, smoking, dying and rebirthing as delicious treats. A meticulously run operation of the highest standard, it's a museum of meat, and we are grateful to delve inside. We place orders to take home and help ourselves to sausage rolls and coffee for the journey back. But I devour mine there and then, in seconds.

Matt drives us back to the station. We're sad to say our goodbyes as we step out of the car, knowing we won't see him for a while and that he took so much time out to show us his life, his world. But just like the sadness of a holiday fling reaching its nadir, Matt has sheep waiting for him and we have a restaurant (and lives, mustn't forget we have lives) to go back to. We're mates now and make plans to see each other next time he's in London. (And we absolutely deliver on our promise: Matt comes in with a date, and we treat him like royalty. It's the least we can do.)

We returned enriched, humbled by our learnings of land, soil and sheep. We are grateful to work with Matt and his wonderful companions and deeply admire his farming methodology. Personal relationships go a long way in business, and Matt being the loveliest bloke with the best farming ethics makes us determined to retain his custom, his mutton and his friendship for years to come.

— Ferhat

THIS
PIECE
OF ART
IS ABOUT
THE
TOILETS
BEING
THIS
← WAY

BABAK GANJEI 21

No Rakı!

The scene is set. A customer, often of Turkish origin, enthusiastically walks in and is greeted by front of house, who gently leads them to their table. They're sat and receive a glass of cold tap water whilst menus are placed in front of them.

The customer scours the drinks list: up-and-down, up-and-down, up-and-down again, like someone rummaging for the keys inside their tote bag after they leave the house and hoping they're not locked out – not again, lesson learnt.

Eyebrows are raised as a confused look permeates their expression. They scan the room, seeking the most-senior-looking server, and ideally the most Turkish in appearance. If I'm in, that person is me. They source me to great relief and gesture me to come over.

I already know how this conversation goes, but I play along, slowly making my way over to the table with great dread and slight annoyance – like a child begrudgingly walking into class even though they want nothing more than to pull a sickie and stay home to watch Cartoon Network all day.

'Excuse me, are you Turkish?' they ask, to which I reply *'Evet'* in the native tongue to avoid confusion. The remaining conversation is translated from Turkish into English.

Customer: 'There's no rakı?'

Me: 'Correct.'

Customer, surprised, laughing somewhat nervously in a state of perplexed irritation: 'Why isn't there any rakı? Is this not a Turkish restaurant?'

Me: 'Because we don't feel it complements the menu and pairs well with what we serve.'

Customer: 'Oh, what?! Are you serious?! How can there not be any rakı for goodness' sake?! Can you pop to the shop (store) and buy some?'

Me: 'Absolutely not. Are you here to eat or to solely drink rakı? Because if rakı is the be-all-end-all part of your dining experience, there are over a dozen other restaurants on this strip catering to that. I, personally, devise the drinks menu, and I am an advocate for mostly low-intervention wines; we have wonderful offerings which I really encourage you try. As well, I don't serve rakı, because I do not love rakı. I only want to serve that in which I believe; the same goes for the food that my brother prepares. This is a personal menu for both of us. I hope you can understand.'

<Ten second pause>

Customer: 'Very well. What's a *Picklerak*?'

Me: 'Well, I suppose I lied because that is rakı, but it's served as a shot with a pickle chaser, much like a Bourbon Pickleback. It's a play on words – it's my invention, and I'm quite proud of it really because...'

Customer, abruptly: 'Very well. Send me one of those but in a tall rakı glass with lots of ice then. Skip the pickle.'

Oh rakı, how I loathe thee! I spent a good decade serving customers when Mangal II was a traditional kebab house and sat for hours as they'd descend into a rakı craze. I'd watch and wait for them to finish up whilst they'd fully get into the rakı groove, slowly sipping and taking baby bites of their food. With rakı, as the culture dictates, you sip and nibble, sip and nibble, lasting hours. A meal would become an enduring four-hour activity, whereby someone would blast old Turkish arabesque music from an iPhone and over the restaurant's playlist. Eventually, this same person would demand we turn our own music off so they can hear theirs. Rakı is a spirit, but the cocktail of it with the wrong consumer leads to an obnoxious and aggressive douchebag. It's a well-known effect, so much so that in Turkey it is called 'Lion's milk', because it prompts courage and fire (or, perhaps, one to behave like a dickhead, you could say?).

Many family BBQs, weddings, birthdays, summer gatherings and New Year's Eves have been tainted or ruined by rakı. Many a restaurant service has descended into a 4 a.m. bedlam of shitpie because of rakı. Forgive me for not loving or embracing this spirit. Forgive me for refusing to serve this spirit in its traditional sense when the turn time per table that we can offer is 1 hour and 45 minutes due to the high demand at our small establishment. Forgive me for not caring about how little I am bending to Turkish culture because I refuse to serve people who will most likely activate their inner arsehole and refuse to enjoy the meal for what it offers, as they mask every plate of food with the strong, pungent anise seed spirit down their guzzle.

Dealt with tastefully, rakı can make a great companion. Paired with salty feta cheese, luminous seasonal melon, fried Mediterranean anchovies or cold garlicky mezze like aubergine yogurt. Even I can come around to that indulgence whenever I'm in Istanbul at a *meyhane* eatery having the time of my life. The anise seed balances these flavours delectably, each small bite is married with a small sip and you get an umami dopamine rush with each pairing. The music is romantic. The conversations are jolly and rambunctious. The flirting is off the roof. The servers are charming and in the zone. The charismatic Gypsy-Romany is in full swing, selling roses to you from the balcony. The buzz. I get it.

But a quick glance at our menu, and you will spot the absence of these dishes. And there are plenty, and I mean plenty, of quality spots within a five-mile radius of Mangal II serving them to an exemplary standard. So, kindly, shoot off and go have your rakı elsewhere. And come back here for a different experience, because we're in north-east London, buddy.

— Ferhat

Leek, Tulum and Caraway Börek

Serves 4–6

For the filling

2 leeks, white parts only,
   halved lengthwise
3 tablespoons olive oil, plus extra
   for brushing
3–4 white onions (500 g/1 lb 2 oz),
   roughly chopped
6–7 cloves garlic, thinly sliced,
   plus 1 clove garlic, minced
250 g/9 oz Tulum cheese
   (*Tulum peyniri*) or Turkish feta
   (*beyaz peynir*)
2 tablespoons white wine vinegar
2 tablespoons lemon juice
Salt, to taste

For the caraway butter

6 tablespoons white wine
300 g/10½ oz butter, melted
1½ teaspoons sea salt
3 tablespoons caraway seeds

Assembly

4 sheets filo pastry, cut lengthwise
   into thirds
1 egg

Filling Preheat a charcoal grill over high heat until the coals are white hot. Brush the leeks with olive oil.

Meanwhile, heat 3 tablespoons of oil in a large frying pan over medium-low heat. Add the onions and sauté for 3 minutes, until caramelized. Add the sliced garlic and sauté for another 2 minutes, until golden. Set aside to cool.

Place the leeks on the grill and grill for 3 minutes on each side, until charred. Transfer them to a baking sheet, then cool. Thinly slice lengthwise.

Put the onion-garlic mixture into a bowl. Add the leeks and the remaining ingredients. Season with salt.

Caraway butter Heat the wine in a pan over medium heat until reduced by half. Reduce the heat to low and slowly stir in the butter and salt. Add the caraway seeds and cook for 2–3 minutes, taking care not to burn the seeds. Set aside.

Assembly Preheat the oven to 170°C/340°F (Gas mark 3). Line a baking sheet with parchment paper.

Lay a sheet of filo onto the prepared baking sheet. Brush the top with the caraway butter. Place another sheet on top, then brush with more caraway butter. Add enough leek mixture to spread out into a thin layer, leaving a 1-cm/½-inch gap along the edges. Roll the filo, lengthwise, to create a log. Shape into a coil. Repeat with the remaining sheets.

In a small bowl, combine the egg and 3 tablespoons of caraway butter and mix well. Brush the coil liberally with the mixture. Bake for 30 minutes, until golden.

KAPYA 3/.
12/10 FM

Ferments

Our vegetable 'waste' ferments are both sweet and sour, thus eliminating the need to use pomegranate molasses, sumac or bottled 'lemon juice' (which is just citric acid with lemon flavouring and commonly used in London-based Turkish restaurants). They can be used as a unique sour flavouring agent in lieu of lemons; we even prepare them as a powder to preserve the same properties and flavour profiles demanded in Turkish food but with a little edge.

Take parsley, for example. Its fibrous stems are often discarded since they aren't regarded as attractive as the leaves are, but when we ferment them with 3% salt, they taste like green olives. We use them in our börek fillings to impart subtle layers of flavour.

Salgam, a hearty, spicy accompaniment of rakı, can be used to dress grilled onion salads. Why not make your own by fermenting beetroots (beets) and carrots? The flavour of home-made salgam is a complex combination of lactic sourness and sweetness – plus, you still have the earthiness of the beetroots, which is rare in mass-produced salgam. Best of all, after you use the juice, you're left with the vegetables – sharp pops of flavour that complement smoked and grilled meats. They cut through the richness and add textural crunch.

— Sertaç

Fermented Vegetables

At the restaurant, we often ferment the surplus or 'trim' from vegetables by preserving them in salt. The mixture is kept at an ambient temperature to develop the bacteria and then refrigerated until the vegetables acquire the desired level of lactic acidity and flavour. This process – introduced to me by the head chef at Broaden and Build, Elliot Bernardo (page 39) – follows the same school of thought as their executive chef Matt Orlando: to reduce waste and prepare a unique product.

Makes 1 kg/2 lbs 4 oz

1 kg/2 lbs 4 oz vegetables such
    as beetroots (beets), peppers
    or parsley stems
2 tablespoons salt

Combine the vegetables and salt in large vacuum bags (or sterilised jars). Mix well. Vacuum or cover your vegetables and leave them somewhere warm to ferment for 10 days. Taste the mixture. If it requires more fermentation time, seal it and set aside for another 1–2 days. Once it's sour enough, store in the refrigerator to stop the fermentation process.

Fermented vegetables can be stored in the refrigerator for up to 3 months.

Grilled Cucumber
and Buttermilk Cacik

Serves 2–4

200 ml (7 fl oz/scant 1 cup)
    buttermilk
1 clove garlic, grated
4 teaspoons lemon juice
Scant 1 teaspoon salt,
    plus extra for sprinkling
½ teaspoon white pepper
1 cucumber
Sunflower oil, for greasing
Dill oil (page 124), for finishing
Black (urfa) chilli flakes,
    for sprinkling

Preheat a charcoal grill over medium heat until the coals are white hot.

In a shallow bowl, combine all the ingredients except the cucumber and oils.

Brush the hot grill with sunflower oil, then sprinkle with salt. Add the whole cucumber and grill for 4–5 minutes, until charred on all sides. Transfer the cucumber to a chopping (cutting) board and slice into large pieces.

Spoon over the buttermilk cacik, finish with dill oil and sprinkle with chilli flakes. Serve.

Mushroom Manti

Serves 4

For the mushroom filling
100 g/3½ oz portobello mushrooms
100 g/3½ oz button
    (white) mushrooms
1 tablespoon sunflower oil,
    plus extra for deep-frying
100 g/3½ oz oyster mushrooms,
    thinly sliced
2 tablespoons chopped onions
2 cloves garlic, minced
2 tablespoons finely chopped parsley
Lemon juice, to taste
Fine salt, to taste

For the dough
200 g (7 oz/1½ cups +
    2 tablespoons) plain (all-purpose)
    flour, plus extra for dusting
¼ teaspoon fine salt

For the yogurt
200 g (7 oz/¾ cup) Turkish
    or Greek yogurt
6–7 cloves garlic, minced
2 teaspoons lemon juice
Fine salt, to taste

For the tomatoes
1–2 vine-ripened tomatoes
1 tablespoon sunflower oil,
    plus extra for brushing
Salt
1 tablespoon chopped onions
2 cloves garlic, minced
3 tablespoons Smoked Olive Oil
    (page 100)

Mushroom filling Preheat the oven to 180°C/350°F (Gas mark 4). Place the portobello and button (white) mushrooms on a baking sheet and roast for 20 minutes.

Heat the oil in a deep fryer or deep pan to 160°C/325°F. Carefully lower the oyster mushrooms into the hot oil and deep-fry for 3–4 minutes, until golden.

Heat a tablespoon of oil in a small frying pan over medium heat. Add the onions and garlic and sauté for 5 minutes, until the onions are translucent.

In a food processor, combine all the mushrooms, the onion mixture and parsley and pulse until minced (do not purée). Season with lemon juice and salt.

Dough In a large bowl, combine the flour and salt and make a well. Slowly pour in 100 ml (3½ fl oz/scant ½ cup) of boiling water, little by little, and mix with a fork for 3 minutes, until the dough comes together.

Transfer the dough to a clean work counter dusted with flour. Using your hands, knead the dough for 10 minutes until smooth. Place the dough into a bowl, cover, and set aside for 30 minutes.

Roll out the dough about 2-mm/¹⁄₁₆-inch thick or pass it through a pasta roller, working your way down from the highest setting. Slice the dough into 5-cm/2-inch squares. Dust with flour, then stack on a plate. Put in an airtight container and refrigerate for 2–4 hours.

Yogurt Combine all the ingredients in a small bowl and mix well.

Tomatoes Preheat a charcoal grill over medium heat until the coals are white hot.

Halve the tomatoes, then brush with the sunflower oil and season with salt. Place them on the grill and grill for 15 minutes, until charred all over. Transfer the tomatoes to a food processor and pulse until broken down.

Heat 1 tablespoon of sunflower oil in a small frying pan over medium heat. Add the onions and garlic and sauté for 5 minutes, until the onions are softened and translucent. Add the tomatoes and smoked olive oil and sauté for another 20 minutes, until reduced by half.

⅂

Assembly

Melted butter, for drizzling

Sweet pepper flakes (*tatlı pul biber*),
    for sprinkling

Dried mint, for sprinkling

Seasonal bitter leaves, wild
    mushrooms or edible flowers,
    for garnish

Assembly Remove the dough wrappers from the refrigerator. Add a heaped teaspoon of mushroom filling to the centre of a wrapper. Pinch the wrapper and join the corners in the centre to resemble an 'x' from above. Place on a baking sheet or large plate and repeat with the remaining filling and wrappers. Freeze the manti for up to 3 months.

Bring a large pan of salted water to boil. Working in batches to avoid overcrowding, carefully lower the manti and cook for 4 minutes.

Meanwhile, spoon the yogurt into 4 serving bowls. Top with the tomato sauce. Using a slotted spoon, carefully transfer the manti to a plate lined with a clean cloth or perforated tray to drain. Place 4 manti into each bowl.

Drizzle with the melted butter and sprinkle over the sweet pepper flakes (*tatlı pul biber*) and dried mint. Garnish with bitter leaves, wild mushrooms or edible flowers. Serve immediately.

Chickpea Fritters with Brown Crab

Serves 6

125 g (4¼ oz/scant 1 cup) chickpea
 flour
120 ml (4 fl oz/½ cup) olive oil
1¼ teaspoons salt, plus extra
 to taste
3 white cabbage leaves, stem
 removed and thinly sliced
4 teaspoons sunflower oil,
 plus extra for frying
100 g/3½ oz brown crab meat
1 teaspoon lemon juice
2 teaspoons extra-virgin olive oil
Black (urfa) chilli flakes
Dill, for garnish
1 lemon wedge, to serve (optional)

In a bowl, combine the chickpea flour and 150 ml (5 fl oz/⅔ cup) of water and mix well.

In a pan, combine the 120 ml (4 fl oz/½ cup) of olive oil and 350 ml (12 fl oz/1½ cups) of water and warm over medium heat. Remove the pan from the heat, then pour in the batter. Using an immersion blender, blend until smooth.

Return the pan to the heat and stir for 15 minutes, until the batter is cooked through. Season with salt.

Line a small tray with parchment paper. Pour in the batter to a depth of 2.5 cm/1 inch. Set aside to cool. Refrigerate for 2 hours, until completely firm. Cut into 6 (2 x 3-cm/¾ x 1¼-inch) portions.

Preheat a charcoal grill over medium heat until the coals are white hot.

Brush the cabbage with the sunflower oil and sprinkle over 1¼ teaspoons of salt. Squeeze out any moisture. Place in a grill basket. Grill for 2 minutes.

In a small bowl, combine the cabbage, crab meat, lemon juice and extra-virgin olive oil and gently mix.

Heat the sunflower oil in a frying pan over medium-high heat to 160°C/325°F. Carefully lower the fritters into the hot oil and deep-fry for 2–3 minutes, turning halfway, until golden brown. Transfer to a paper towel–lined plate to drain.

Place the fritters on a serving platter, top with the crab mixture and black (urfa) chilli flakes. Garnish with dill and serve with a lemon wedge, if desired.

Mackerel and Vine Leaf Sarma

Serves 2

6 brined vine leaves, stems removed
2 mackerel fillets, pinbones removed
Sunflower oil, for brushing
100 g/3½ oz butter
3½ tablespoons Smoked Olive Oil
   (page 100)
1 teaspoon sweet pepper flakes
   (*tatlı pul biber*)

Overlap 3 vine leaves on a clean work counter. Repeat with the other 3 vine leaves. Place the mackerel in the centre, skin-side down, and roll the vine leaf over the mackerel, tucking in the sides. Repeat with the other vine leaves and mackerel. Refrigerate for a day. The salt from the brine leaves should dry out the leaves and cure the mackerel.

Preheat a charcoal grill (or cast-iron grill) over medium heat until the coals are white hot. Oil the vine-wrapped fillets and place on the grill. Sear for 30 seconds on each side. Meanwhile, in a frying pan, combine the butter, smoked olive oil and sweet pepper flakes (*tatlı pul biber*). Heat over medium-high heat until the mixture starts to foam.

Transfer the mackerel onto 2 serving plates. Spoon over the foaming butter and serve hot.

Mackerel in Fried Vine Leaf

Serves 3

Peel of 1 orange
½ Sivri pepper
200 ml (7 fl oz/scant 1 cup)
    sunflower oil, plus extra for frying
6 brined vine leaves, patted dry
    and stems removed
1 large mackerel fillet, pinbones
    removed
2 teaspoons sweet pepper flakes
    (*tatlı pul biber*)

In a high-powered blender, combine the orange peel, Sivri pepper and oil and blend until the blender feels hot. (The heat will infuse the fruits and vegetables with natural flavours and release their oils.) Set aside to infuse overnight. Line a fine-mesh sieve with muslin (cheesecloth) and place it into a bowl. Strain the mixture.

Preheat a charcoal grill over medium heat until the coals are white hot.

Heat the sunflower oil in a deep fryer or deep pan to 170ºC/340ºF. Add the dried vine leaves, shiny side down, and deep-fry for 30 seconds. Flip and deep-fry for another 30 seconds. Carefully transfer to a wire rack lined with paper towels to drain.

Add the mackerel to the grill, skin-side down. Give the grate a tap every 10–20 seconds to prevent the mackerel from sticking to it. Grill for 5 minutes, until the skin has caramelized. Transfer the mackerel to a chopping (cutting) board and set aside to cook in the residual heat.

Slice the mackerel into 3 pieces. Drizzle with the orange oil and sprinkle over sweet pepper flakes (*tatlı pul biber*). Place on top of the vine leaves on 3 serving plates. Serve at room temperature.

Brown Crab and Rice Sarma
with Shellfish Emulsion

Baldo rice is extremely starchy. Be sure to rinse the rice continuously until the water runs clear. Alternatively, soak the grains overnight.

Serves 4

For the brown crab and rice sarma
Olive oil, for frying
100 g (3½ oz/½ cup) baldo rice,
    well rinsed
200 ml (7 fl oz/scant 1 cup) smoked
    fish stock
100 g/3½ oz brown crab meat
3 tablespoons finely chopped dill
2 tablespoons finely chopped parsley
2 tablespoons butter,
    room temperature
Lemon juice, to taste
Fine salt, to taste
200 g/7 oz brined vine leaves,
    stems removed

For the shellfish emulsion
150 g/5½ oz shells from
    langoustines, prawns (shrimp)
    or lobster
150 ml (5 fl oz/⅔ cup) vegetable oil
1 medium (US large) egg yolk
2 teaspoons ground cumin
Lemon juice, to taste
Fine salt, to taste

Assembly
1 tablespoon black (urfa) chilli flakes
1 tablespoon Aleppo chilli flakes
1 tablespoon coriander seeds
1 tablespoon fennel seeds
Lemon wedges, to serve

Brown crab and rice sarma Heat the oil in a pan over medium-high heat. Add the rice and sauté for 3–4 minutes, until the grains are toasted. Pour in the fish stock and bring to a boil. Reduce the heat to medium-low and simmer for 10 minutes, covered, until the rice is cooked. Remove the pan from the heat, keep covered and steam for another 30 minutes.

Fold in the crab meat, dill, parsley and butter. Season with lemon juice and salt.

Place a spoon of the mixture on a vine leaf. Roll the leaf, tucking in the sides as you go along. Set aside.

Preheat a charcoal grill over high heat until the coals are white hot.

Shellfish emulsion Preheat the oven to 160°C (325°F/Gas mark 3).

Place the shells on a baking sheet and roast for 20 minutes. Transfer the mixture to a high-power blender and add the oil. Blend until smooth. Strain through a sieve lined with muslin (cheesecloth).

In a blender, combine 150 ml (5 fl oz/⅔ cup) of the shellfish oil, the egg yolk and cumin and blend until emulsified. Season with lemon juice and salt.

Assembly Combine the spices in a spice grinder (or use a pestle and mortar). Grind to a powder.

Add the stuffed vine leaves to the grill and grill for 3–4 minutes, until all sides are well charred. Transfer the vine leaves to a serving plate. Add the shellfish emulsion on top and dust over the spice blend.

Serve immediately with lemon wedges.

Spiced Quail

Serves 4

For the quail
400 ml (14 fl oz/1⅔ cups) buttermilk
1½ tablespoons salt
1½ teaspoons sugar
½ teaspoon sweet pepper flakes
    (*tatlı pul biber*)
1 teaspoon black pepper
1 teaspoon ground cumin
½ teaspoon dried oregano
4 quails, spatchcocked

For the spice blend
4 tablespoons fennel seeds
3½ tablespoons dried oregano
2½ tablespoons ground cumin
1½ tablespoons Aleppo chilli flakes
2 teaspoons black (urfa) chilli flakes

Quail Combine all the ingredients except the quails in a large bowl. Pour in 100 ml (3½ fl oz/scant ½ cup) of water. Using an immersion blender, mix well. Add the quails, cover and refrigerate for 12 hours to brine.

Shake off the excess mixture from the quails. Transfer them to a wire rack set over a baking sheet and refrigerate for 6–24 hours.

Spice blend Combine the spices in a spice grinder (or use a pestle and mortar). Grind to a powder.

Preheat a charcoal grill over high heat until the coals are white hot.

Skewer through the breast and legs of each quail. Grill, breast-side down, over medium heat for 5 minutes to sear. Flip over and grill for another 4–5 minutes, until just cooked through. Transfer to a plate and set aside to rest for 6 minutes.

Dust the spice blend over the quails. Serve hot.

Sweetbreads in Pomegranate Molasses

Serves 2

½ onion, chopped
2 cloves garlic, chopped
1½ teaspoons salt
300 ml (10 fl oz/1¼ cups) milk
200 g/7 oz lamb sweetbreads
Sunflower oil, for brushing
2 tablespoons hot melted butter
4 teaspoons pomegranate molasses
4 teaspoons Smoked Olive Oil
   (page 100)
4 teaspoons dried oregano
4 teaspoons ground cumin
2 teaspoons sweet pepper flakes
   (tatlı pul biber)
Store-bought or home-made Pide
   (page 120), to serve (optional)
Grilled lettuce, to serve

In a bowl, combine the onions, garlic, salt and milk. Add the sweetbreads to the brine and refrigerate for 12 hours.

Drain the sweetbreads. Set aside for another 4 hours.

Preheat a charcoal grill over high heat until the coals are white hot. Brush the sweetbreads with sunflower oil, then skewer them onto thin skewers. Place on the grill and grill for 8 minutes, until caramelized.

Transfer the sweetbreads to a bowl. Add the remaining ingredients and mix well.

Place the bread, if using, into a shallow serving bowl. Add the sweetbread mixture. Serve with grilled lettuce.

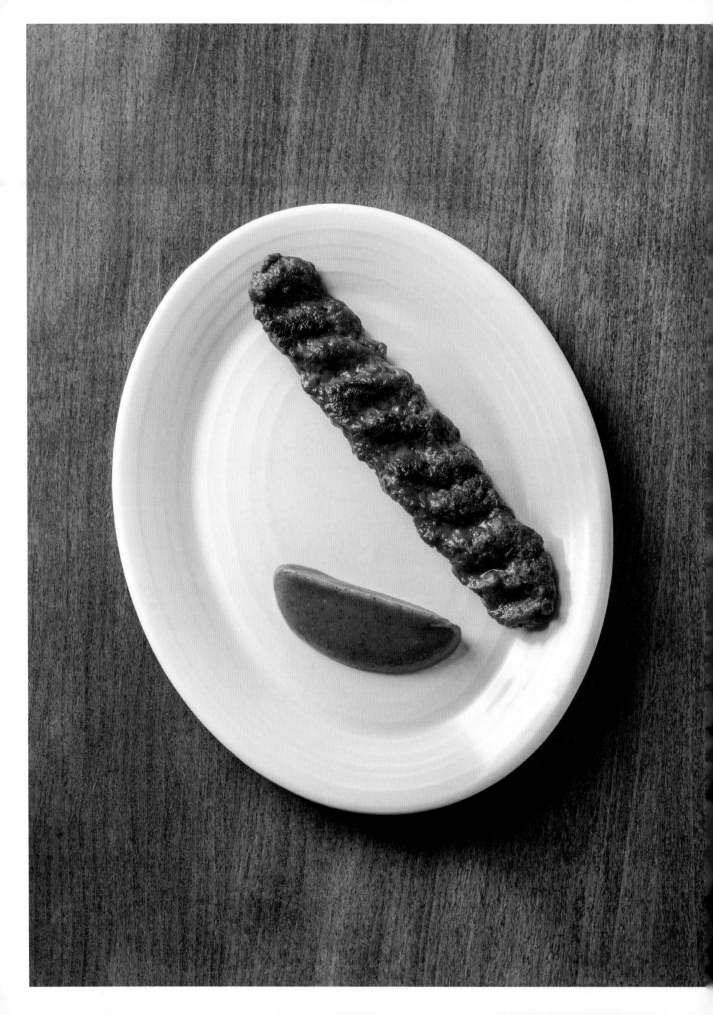

Cull Yaw Köfte with Grilled Apple Sauce

Cull yaw is a type of free-roaming, retired mutton, coined by Matt Chatfield, the founder of the Cornwall Project (page 143).

Due to the strong smoky nature that mangal imparts on meats, we devised a sauce that would act as a subtle counterpart. A sauce like ketchup but made from grilled apples was ideal. Sweet, tart and smoky, this impactful condiment is the perfect alternative to classic Turkish sauces. You can use it to accompany gamey or heavy meat flavours.

Serves 12

For the grilled apple sauce
250 g/9 oz red apples, cored
Olive oil, for brushing
2 tablespoons sunflower oil
¼ white onion, sliced
2 cloves garlic, sliced
120 ml (4 fl oz/½ cup)
    white wine vinegar
125 g (4½ oz/½ cup)
    dark brown sugar

For the cull yaw köfte
700 g/1 lb 9 oz mutton rump
250 g/9 oz mutton fat
2½ tablespoons sea salt
4 teaspoons ground cumin
1 tablespoon sweet paprika
1 teaspoon sweet pepper flakes
    (tatlı pul biber)

Grilled apple sauce Preheat a charcoal grill over high heat until the coals are white hot. Brush the olive oil over the apples, then place them on the hot grill. Grill for 10 minutes on each side, until charred.

Heat the sunflower oil in a medium pan over high heat. Add the onions and garlic and sauté for 3–5 minutes, until caramelized. Add the apples. Stir in the vinegar and sugar. Reduce the heat to medium and cook for 30 minutes, mashing occasionally.

Transfer the mixture to a blender and purée until smooth. Strain through a fine-mesh sieve and set aside to cool.

Cull yaw köfte Freeze the mutton rump and fat for 1 hour.

Preheat a charcoal grill over high heat until the coals are white hot.

Pass the fat through a meat grinder. Then pass it again with the mutton rump. (Alternatively, finely chop both.) Add the remaining ingredients, then use your hands to mix until the mixture is uniform in colour.

Weigh out the mixture into 80-g/2¾-oz portions and roll into balls. Then, using your thumb, make indentations along the meat to create the classic köfte shape. Repeat with the remaining mixture.

Place the skewers on the hot grill and grill for 3–4 minutes on each side, until the meat is cooked through and nicely charred.

Transfer to a plate and serve immediately with a quenelle of grilled apple sauce.

Rakı Baba

Serves 6

For the baba
5 g/⅛ oz fast-action
   (active dry) yeast
2 tablespoons milk
600 g (1 lb 5 oz/3¾ cups) strong
   white flour, plus extra for dusting
4 tablespoons caster
   (superfine) sugar
12 chilled medium (US large) eggs,
   lightly beaten
Pinch of fine salt
200 g (7 oz/1¾ sticks) butter,
   cubed, room temperature,
   plus extra for greasing

For the syrup
200 g (7 oz/1 cup) sugar
1½ tablespoons rakı

Assembly
300 g/10½ oz Cultured Kaymak
   (page 102) or clotted cream
Edible flowers, for garnish (optional)

Baba In a small bowl, combine the yeast, milk and 3 tablespoons of flour and mix until it forms a smooth ball. Wrap the bowl in clingfilm (plastic wrap), then set aside to rise in a warm place for 30 minutes, or until doubled in size.

In a stand mixer fitted with the paddle attachment, combine the remaining flour and yeast mixture and mix on medium-low speed for 3–5 minutes. Add the sugar and eggs and mix for 20 minutes, until the dough is elastic and comes away from the side of the bowl.

Switch to the hook attachment. Turn the mixer back on, then add the salt. Mix in the butter, a cube at a time, ensuring that the cube is fully incorporated before adding the next one. Once all the butter has been added, work the dough for another 10 minutes, until soft and pale yellow.

Remove the bowl from the stand mixer. Cover it with clingfilm, then leave the dough to rise in a warm place for 3 hours, until doubled in size.

Preheat the oven to 180°C/350°F (Gas mark 4). Grease and flour 6 baba moulds.

Knock back the dough. Weight out 70-g/2½-oz pieces and place them into the moulds. Set aside in a warm place for 3 hours, until the dough expands into each mould and forms a dome. Bake for 30–35 minutes, until deeply golden brown. Set aside for 10 minutes to cool. Invert the cakes onto a wire rack to cool completely.

Syrup Combine all the ingredients in a pan. Add 200 ml (7 fl oz/ scant 1 cup) of water and heat until the sugar has dissolved and the syrup is warmed through. Remove from the heat.

Assembly Whip the cultured kaymak until still peaks form. Put the whipped kaymak into a piping bag. (Skip this step if using clotted cream.)

Using tongs, dip a baba into the syrup, turning it around, until coated on all sides. Gently squeeze out the excess syrup, then transfer the soaked baba to a cooling rack set over a baking sheet, turning occasionally to evenly soak. Repeat with the remaining babas. Pipe the whipped kaymak onto the plate (or add a dollop of clotted cream). Garnish with edible flowers, if desired.

Mountain Tea Ice Cream with Rhubarb and Grilled Filo Cracker

Serves 4–6

For the mountain tea ice cream
1 gelatine sheet
500 ml (17 fl oz/generous 2 cups) double (heavy) cream
500 ml (17 fl oz/ generous 2 cups) milk
100 g (3½ oz/½ cup) caster (superfine) sugar
2½ tablespoons ground mountain tea (sideritis)
9 egg yolks (180 g/6 oz)
120 ml (4 fl oz/½ cup) glucose

For the rhubarb compote
200 g/7 oz rhubarb, sliced into 1-cm/½-inch pieces
2 tablespoons sugar
1½ tablespoons light brown sugar
2 teaspoons lemon juice
Pinch of sea salt

For the grilled filo cracker
500 g (1 lb 2 oz/2¼ cups) light brown sugar
200 g (7 oz/1¾ sticks) butter
2 teaspoons sea salt
300 ml (10 fl oz/1¼ cups) apple juice
1 sheet filo pastry

Mountain tea ice cream In a small bowl, bloom the gelatine in water. Remove and place in a bowl.

Combine the cream and milk in a large pan and bring to a slow simmer. Hold it at 80°C/175°F.

Meanwhile, in a large bowl, combine the sugar, mountain tea (sideritis) and egg yolks and whisk until aerated and thickened. Slowly whisk in the milk mixture, then pour the mixture back into the pan. Add the glucose and bloomed gelatine. Slowly cook over medium heat, whisking frequently, until the mixture reaches 82°C/180°F. Strain through a fine-mesh sieve, then set aside to cool.

Rhubarb compote In a pan, combine the rhubarb and sugars. Add 1 tablespoon of water and cook over low heat for 10 minutes, until the sugars have macerated the rhubarb and it reaches your desired texture. Finish with lemon juice and salt, then transfer the compote to a bowl. Refrigerate until needed.

Grilled filo cracker In a large pan, combine the sugar, butter, salt and apple juice. Cook over medium heat for 5 minutes, until caramelized. Set aside at room temperature to prevent the apple caramel from splitting. If it does split, simply whisk it over medium heat.

Trim the filo into 20 x 10-cm/8 x 4-inch sheets. Using a pastry brush, brush with the apple caramel. Fold in half into squares and set them a single layer on a sheet of parchment paper.

Preheat a charcoal grill over medium heat and set a cast-iron grate on top. Once the coals are white hot, add the filo and grill each for a minute, until caramelized. Set aside for 5 minutes, until hardened.

Assembly Place a generous scoop of ice cream into a bowl. Spoon some compote to the side and top with a grilled filo cracker.

Carob Cake with Kaymak Dulce de Leche

Serves 6

For the carob cake
450 g (1 lb/2¼ cups) sugar
8 eggs
450 ml (15 fl oz/scant 2 cups)
    vegetable oil
175 ml (6 fl oz/¾ cup)
    carob molasses
3½ tablespoons Smoked Olive Oil
    (page 100)
620 g (1 lb 6 oz/4 cups plus
    2 tablespoons) plain
    (all-purpose) flour
2¼ teaspoons bicarbonate of soda
    (baking soda)
1 teaspoon salt
1 teaspoon ground cinnamon
Fresh berries, to serve (optional)

For the kaymak dulce de leche
250 g (9 oz/1 cup plus 1 tablespoon)
    brown sugar
150 g (5½ oz/¾ cup) sugar
500 ml (17 fl oz/
    generous 2 cups) milk
100 g (3½ oz/½ cup) Cultured
    Kaymak (page 102)
¼ teaspoon bicarbonate of soda

Carob cake Preheat the oven to 200ºC/400ºF (Gas mark 6). Line a baking dish with parchment paper.

In a stand mixer fitted with the whisk attachment, combine the sugar and eggs. Mix well, then pour in the vegetable oil, carob molasses and smoked olive oil. Mix again.

Sift in the flour, bicarbonate of soda (baking soda), salt and cinnamon. Using a spatula, fold the batter until well mixed. Pour the batter into the prepared baking dish. Reduce the oven temperature to 175ºC/345ºF (Gas mark 4). Bake for 30–35 minutes, until a knife inserted into the centre comes out clean. Set aside for 20 minutes to cool.

Kaymak dulce de leche In a pan, combine the sugars and 400 ml (14 fl oz/1⅔ cups) of water. Heat over medium-high heat, until amber in colour and the sugars begin to caramelize.

Remove the pan from the heat. Carefully fold in the milk, cultured kaymak and bicarbonate of soda. Set aside to cool slightly.

Assembly Slice the carob cake into squares, then serve with the warm kaymak dulce de leche and, if desired, fresh berries.

PROGRESSION
Creations and Reinventions

Fully formed and finally accepted within the community...
We've reached a point where things have settled. At the time
of this book's publication, we celebrated our thirtieth year
of business. We have a completely new outlook on what we
should be serving. Seasonality is at the forefront, like the best
spots in Turkey, and certain dishes may only appear in the
short period while they're in season.

The restaurant has become an adaptable space to suit the
growing seasons. The menu is defined: one half comprising
established favourites and the other half constantly
changing, week to week. We work with the best suppliers in
England with complete traceability. For example, day-boat
fishermen send line-caught fish within twenty-four hours
of catching them. Mature, eight-year-old dairy sheep enjoy
a long retirement in Cornwall before they're culled. They
are dry-aged for forty-five days and lose their farmy sheep
flavour – this is the Mangalica of mutton. Our vegetables are
grown in Kent and Oxfordshire, including tomatoes, peppers,
aubergines (eggplants), courgettes (zucchini), squash, chicory
and carrots.

This is how they operate in Turkey – it isn't a new concept
but, as purveyors, we are responsible for sourcing correctly.
It makes the most sense, and there's no reason why we
shouldn't be doing the same here.

— Sertaç

Recipes

Wine and Dine with Me

You can find me on the floor. I'll be weaving and sliding past tightly packed tables, sucking in my dad belly as I brush past whilst still managing to step on a long coat that's hanging off a chair like a peeled banana skin.

I'll crack the same jokes because, hey, it's your first time here and, as far as you know, it's an original quip. My obsession? Tidying bits and pieces from guests' tables so only what is needed remains. (Farewell empty plate! Adios glass with a seabed of natural wine sediment!) That and refilling water. I can't stop. I won't stop. Stay hydrated, folks! You're in Mangal II – quenching is our quest.

I love service. I love moving; I always have. As a person who struggles to sit still and smell the roses, I relish the uncorking of a wine bottle and smelling the rosé. To sell a bottle of something I adore to customers is one of my greatest joys. To receive positive feedback from guests and validation of my recommendation, for them to agree with my tasting note suggestions, is wholly satisfying.

We have a unique space here. Arched ceiling, rustic décor. Neat touches but also chipped paint and uneven floors so the tables wobble a little here and there despite the best efforts of our table-stoppers. All breathed into life by the visible open kitchen ocakbaşı at the back. The vibrancy of the Mangal II service floor is palpable and incomparable to elsewhere. Every evening, there is a buzz, as we front of house move from section to section like skipping stones, elegantly bouncing off each table with the smallest murmur and maximum visual joy.

I employ front of house servers based off their personality. If you went to a service finishing school somewhere and embody a stuffy, stoic, rigid patter here to our customers – honestly, with all respect – it's not going to happen. You can't train charm, and you can't buy charisma. You either have 'it' or you don't. My team must reflect my restaurant's personality and, by extension, my own. I'm not saying I have all these attributes in all aspects of life. See me at the GPs and you will find a grouchy man with greying hair, reading his book, and huffing and puffing because it's taking ages. I'm not carefree; I don't do festivals or mass gatherings. My idea of hell is clubbing. I romanticise the idea of one day living as a recluse in a cabin somewhere. But on the service floor, for a few hours a night, I switch it on. I switch it on effortlessly because, from the age of fourteen, I have been interacting with guests and have formed skills that allow me to drop all my inhibitions and sadness and fears and put on a performance. There is very, very little difference between working front of house and being a stage actor. You rehearse the menu; the spotlight is on you. You can make or break someone's evening with your gestures and expressions. You have lines to repeat to the audience. You are a pumped-up caricature of yourself. You are addicted to the adrenaline and feed off the room's energy. Pure theatre.

My love of service is married with my other muse, wine. Being able to couple these two virtues fills me with immense excitement every time I work a shift. And what is it about the latter that I find so endearing? Well, within the deep dive into wine I have discovered parallels with myself. I'm sensitive and astute, by nature. The nuances of wine arouse me more than they should. From flavours of dark chocolate, eucalyptus, lychee or buttered toast to aromas of freshly ground hazelnut, coffee beans, rosemary or my grandfather's farmyard barn in Turkey, wine evokes a personal reaction. Wine is complex, with the vines positioning over a hill, the chosen harvest time, the fermentation method, the intricate journey from the soil to your glass. I appreciate it. And yet, it's also not so complicated: wine is either good or shit. I trust my instinct when selecting wines for our menu. I've not had much formal training, and a huge part of me is hesitant to know too much about the different appellations and vintages. Deep down, I feel it will skew my decision-making and take away my childlike curiosity, naivety and joy. Every wine on our list has character, like our front-of-house heroes on the floor, and every bottle is carefully selected to complement the smoky, sour, fat-enveloping and delicate burst of acidity flavour our food menu offers. They can't be too polished, too rigid, too proud, too pretentious. Nope. That's not the Mangal II way.

I will not choose a wine just because it tastes good; it should work well with the food. When tasting wines (and, my word, I sample over a hundred wines a month for work, thanks to our endless supply of importers, many of whom I consider friends), I experience its flavour and effect, but I'm also calculating costing, its positioning in the menu, its pairing with our food. I'm questioning if I like the supplier enough to work with them and if I can afford to add ANOTHER Chardonnay to the menu (in short: yes, always). I'm considering if the wine is from a region I want to promote, if anyone else sells it, and if I need to swallow this one rather than spit it out because it's too good to waste.

I like to select wines from countries that haven't been championed like the French or Italians. I'm a sucker for Slovakian Riesling, Greek

Assyrtiko, Hungarian Tokaji, Turkish Pinot Noir. The snobbery of wine is insufferable, and if I can put a low-intervention Balkan wine on my menu because it's delicious and works for the menu, I promote it without reservation.

This book is filled with outstanding recipes. They deserve all the accolades and attention they've received. We're also loved for our eclectic, well-priced wine list – unanimously praised by fans and critics after I started taking wine seriously. I cannot emphasise enough how proud that makes me, a Turkish kid from London who never went to vineyards or had wine served at the family dinner table. No trips to Bordeaux for the Diriks. No cellars in our Dalston council flat. I worked my arse off tasting and tasting and thinking and sometimes saying something silly to a more knowledgeable person at a trade event, persisting with my opinion that – contrary to all you snooty people in this room – THIS FUCKING WINE TASTES LIKE SUNDRIED TOMATOES TO ME!

And, you know, our service is a bit like that, too. It's elegant and structured with some order, but it's also a little freestyle. Our servers can flit in and out of sections with fluidity. They're encouraged to speak to the guest, engage and leave a little of their personality on the table as a side dish. They're funny; they're witty; they're confident; they're real. Looking down at a guest, mistreating a customer and making someone feel uncomfortable, or worse, unwelcome, is the greatest and most intolerable taboo at Mangal II. It just simply won't happen here. We used to emphasise a 'no dickheads' policy whenever we posted a job vacancy. Whilst we don't use as much colourful language nowadays (because, you know, professionalism) that ethos remains completely true today. We don't employ dickheads, and if someone slowly shows signs of dickheadity, they won't remain here. The service is an extension of that proud core value we embed. And this spills over to the wines we choose. No fancy-pants 1985 vintage of plonk here (though there's absolutely nothing wrong with that). It's just not the Mangal II way. We serve delicious, thought-provoking, fairly-priced wines many of which are made from native grape varieties that are uncommon.

All this makes me proud of working our service floor. It makes every shift so rewarding, working with colleagues whom I'm close to, whose energy I feed off and who feed off mine. Cracking jokes and smiling through a six-hour Tuesday night shift as guests engage and wine is topped up; I am in heaven.

— Ferhat

Beef Ezme

This dish is inspired by the tartare and Turkish *ciğ köfte* –
a raw lamb dish that is kneaded for hours with spices and
bulgur, then served in lettuce with a squeeze of lemon.
It combines the best of British produce with the same sour
Turkish flavors of an ezme salad on a crisp lettuce boat.
A great summer dish.

Serves 2–4

80 g/2¾ oz aged beef fillet tail
10 g/¼ oz smoked mutton fat
    70 g/2½ oz Ezme (page 46)
1 teaspoon Smoked Olive Oil
    (page 100)
1 teaspoon molasses
Gem lettuce leaves

Freeze the beef fillet and mutton fat for 2 hours, until frozen.
Finely dice into uniform pieces. Combine in a bowl, then fold in
the ezme, smoked olive oil and molasses.

Serve in a cold serving bowl with lettuce cups. Enjoy.

Lokma Kebab with Fermented Green Tomato

Lokma kebab is mutton prepared in a medallion or porchetta shape. If your cut of lamb or mutton is on the fatty side, trim it to a thickness of 1 cm/½ inch, which will ensure proper and even cooking.

Serves 4

1 mutton or lamb loin or saddle
    with tenderloin
200 g/7 oz fermented green
    tomatoes (page 158),
    finely chopped
½ Sivri pepper, finely chopped
½ teaspoon sugar
½ teaspoon rice wine vinegar
3½ tablespoons honey
20 g/¾ oz fennel fronds
Ezme (page 46), to serve

Preheat a charcoal grill over high heat until the coals are white hot. Set a cast-iron grate on top.

Separate the tenderloin from the loin. Debone the cut. Place the tenderloin on top of the thinner side of your loin, then roll them. Secure the joints by skewering them together with two wooden skewers in an 'x' formation, running 2.5 cm/1 inch apart.

Slice the loin into 2.5-cm/1-inch pieces, keeping the skewers intact.

In a bowl, combine the tomatoes, peppers, sugar and vinegar. Set aside in a warm location to macerate.

Combine the honey and fennel fronds in a pan and cook over medium-low heat for 5 minutes. Transfer the fennel honey to a metal bowl set in a deep tray with hay. Burn the hay, then cover the bowl with foil to smoke for 10–15 minutes.

Place the lamb on the grill and sear each side for a minute. Transfer to a plate to rest for 3 minutes. Grill again for 20–30 seconds. Set aside again to rest, away from the heat.

Transfer to a serving plate and serve immediately with a spoon of the tomato mixture, ezme and smoked fennel honey.

Grilled Aubergines with Mushroom Broth and Almonds

Serves 4

300 g/10½ oz portobello
　mushrooms
2 cloves garlic
100 g/3½ oz kombu
4 teaspoons ground cumin
2 teaspoons Aleppo chilli flakes
5 almonds (optional)
2 aubergines (eggplants)
Fine salt
Extra-virgin olive oil
Parsley oil (page 206), for drizzling
　(see Note)

Preheat the oven to 180°C/350°F (Gas mark 4). Place the mushrooms on a baking sheet and roast for 20 minutes.

In a large pan, combine the roasted mushrooms, garlic, kombu, cumin and chilli flakes. Pour in 500 ml (17 fl oz/generous 2 cups) of water and bring to a boil. Reduce the heat to medium-low and simmer for 30 minutes. Strain through a fine-mesh sieve, pressing down on the mushrooms and garlic to extract all the liquid.

If using the almonds, heat a small frying pan over medium-high heat. Add the almonds and toast for 1–2 minutes, until lightly brown on both sides. Remove from the heat, then finely chop.

Preheat a charcoal grill over high heat until the coals are white hot. Add the aubergines (eggplants) and grill until charred on all sides. Using tongs, transfer the aubergines to a chopping (cutting) board. Carefully peel the aubergines while they're still hot so their pale green colour is retained. Chop into 1-cm/½-inch pieces. Season with salt and olive oil.

Pour over the broth, drizzle with the parsley oil, if desired, and top with the toasted almonds. Serve hot.

Note: In order to remove all the water from the parsley oil, place the emulsion in the freezer for 1½ hours, until the parsley liquid is frozen. As the water freezes before the oil, pour out the oil and place in the fridge. Discard the water.

Sucuk

Makes 20 sausages

625 g/1 lb 6 oz minced (ground)
 lamb (25% fat)
625 g/1 lb 6 oz minced (ground) beef
 (25% fat)
6–7 cloves garlic, minced
2 tablespoons ground cumin
2 tablespoons black pepper
1⅔ tablespoons fine salt
2½ teaspoons smoked paprika
1½ tablespoons dried oregano
2 teaspoons sweet pepper flakes
 (*tatlı pul biber*)
Pinch of pink salt
Splash of Smoked Olive Oil
 (page 100)
1 metre/3 ft sheep casing,
 about 2.5-cm/1-inch diameter
Sunflower oil, for frying

Combine the lamb and beef in a large bowl. Fold in the remaining ingredients except the sunflower oil and add a splash of water. Mix well.

Pull the casing over the sausage attachment. Tie the other end, then fill the casing with the mixture. Create 20-cm/8-inch sausages and hang for 2 days in the refrigerator to dry.

Heat the sunflower oil in a large frying pan (or grill) over high heat. Add the sucuk and pan-fry for 5 minutes, until cooked through.

Mackerel with Bulgur and Pistachios

Serves 4

For the mackerel and bone butter
4 whole mackerels, cleaned and
    filleted with spines reserved
Pine wood, for smoking
3 cloves garlic, minced
1 sprig oregano
200 g/7 oz butter
4 tablespoons Smoked Olive Oil
    (page 100)

For the bulgur wheat
3½ tablespoons Smoked Olive Oil
    (page 100)
200 g (7 oz/generous 1 cup) bulgur
    wheat
240 ml (8 fl oz/1 cup) roasted
    chicken stock
3 tablespoons butter (optional)
50 g (1¾ oz/⅓ cup) toasted
    pistachios

Assembly
Vegetable oil, for deep-frying
2 yellow peaches

Mackerel and bone butter Place your mackerel bones in a metal bowl and set in a large metal tray next to some pine. Reserve the mackerel for assembly. Torch the pine to smoke and cover the tray with aluminium foil. Smoke for 15 minutes.

In a pan, combine the mackerel bones, garlic, oregano, butter and smoked olive oil. Cook over medium heat for 10 minutes.

Transfer the mixture to a blender and blend until smooth. Set aside for 2 hours to infuse.

Line a fine-mesh sieve with muslin (cheesecloth) and place it over a bowl. Pour in the butter and strain.

Bulgur wheat Heat the smoked olive oil in a pan over medium heat. Add the bulgur and sauté for 3–4 minutes, until toasted. This process will impart more flavour into your wheat. Pour in the roasted chicken stock and bring to a boil. Reduce the heat to medium-low, cover and simmer for 13 minutes. Set aside for 30 minutes.

If desired, stir in the butter for a creamier bulgur. Mix in the pistachios.

Assembly Preheat a charcoal grill over high heat until the coals are white hot. Set a cast-iron grate on top.

Heat oil in a deep fryer to 160°C/325°F. Add the peaches and deep-fry for 3 minutes, until the skins come away from the flesh. Fill a bowl with iced water. Add the peaches to shock them. Drain, then peel the peach skins. Split them in half, remove the stone (pit) and thinly slice.

Grill the mackerel, skin-side down. Give the grate a tap every 10–20 seconds to prevent the mackerel from sticking to it. Grill for 5 minutes, until the skin has caramelized. Transfer the mackerel to a plate and set aside to cook in the residual heat.

To serve, spoon warm bulgur into serving bowls. Lay the peach slices to one side, place a mackerel over top and finish with the clarified mackerel butter. Serve immediately.

Çökelek with Braised Asparagus

Serves 6

For the çökelek
1 kg (2 lbs 4 oz/4½ cups) Turkish
   or Greek yogurt
200 ml (7 fl oz/scant 1 cup) milk
2¼ teaspoons fine salt
1 tablespoon lemon juice

For the braised asparagus
5–6 asparagus
100 g/3½ oz mint
100 g/3½ oz parsley
1 teaspoon salt
300 ml (10 fl oz/1¼ cups)
   sunflower oil
2 teaspoons lemon juice
Salt, to taste

For the nettles
1 cup nettle leaves
3 tablespoons white vinegar
Grapeseed oil, for frying

Assembly
Garlic flowers, for garnish

Çökelek In a large pan, combine the yogurt and milk. Slowly bring to a boil over medium heat, stirring the mixture with a spatula to prevent it from catching. Boil for 3 minutes, then stir in the salt and lemon juice. Simmer for 20 minutes, stirring occasionally, until it splits and curds begin to form.

Line a fine-mesh sieve with muslin (cheesecloth) and place it over a bowl. Pour in the mixture and leave it to strain overnight in the refrigerator.

Braised asparagus Bring a pan of salted water to a boil. Add the asparagus and cook for 2 minutes. Fill a bowl with iced water. Transfer the asparagus to the ice bath. Drain.

Trim the woody ends of the asparagus, then finely slice into circles all the way up until the tips.

In a blender, combine the mint, parsley, salt and oil and blend until smooth. Steep for 1 hour, then strain the mixture.

Fold the asparagus into the mint oil. Add the lemon juice and salt.

Nettles In a large bowl, combine the nettle leaves and vinegar. Add 1 L (34 fl oz/4¼ cups) of water and set aside for 2 hours. Drain, then pat dry thoroughly.

Heat the oil in a deep fryer or deep pan to 160°C/325°F. Carefully lower the nettle leaves into the oil and deep-fry each side for 1 minute. Transfer to a paper towel–lined plate to drain.

Assembly To serve, spoon the çökelek onto a plate and make a well. Top with asparagus, 2 fried nettle leaves and garlic flowers. Serve.

Fermented Pepper Sarma with Parsley

Sarma, meaning 'wrapped' in Turkish, is the common term for stuffed grape leaves, vine leaves or cabbage leaves.

Baldo rice is extremely starchy. Be sure to rinse the rice continuously until the water runs clear. Alternatively, soak the grains overnight.

Serves 4

For the fermented Kapya pepper
1 large Kapya pepper or red
   bell pepper, stemmed, halved
   lengthwise, seeded and deveined
   (150 g/5½ oz)
¾ teaspoon salt

For the parsley oil
1 bunch parsley
500 ml (17 fl oz/generous 2 cups)
   sunflower oil
3 cloves garlic
4 egg yolks
2 teaspoons white wine vinegar
Salt, to taste
Lemon juice, to taste

For the filling
2 tablespoons olive oil
1 large white onion, finely chopped
2–3 cloves garlic, minced
400 g (14 oz/2⅓ cups) baldo rice,
   well rinsed
1 head savoy cabbage

Fermented Kapya pepper Combine the ingredients in a bowl and mix well. Add the peppers to a vacuum bag (or a sterilised glass jar) and seal tightly. Ferment in a warm location for 7–10 days. Once the peppers have your desired acidity and sweetness, refrigerate for up to 3 months.

Transfer the peppers to a blender and purée until smooth.

Parsley oil Bring a pan of salted water to a boil. Meanwhile, fill a bowl with iced water. Add the parsley to the pan and blanch for 5 seconds. Transfer the parsley to the ice bath to shock it and release its colour.

In a blender, combine the parsley and oil. Blend until the blender begins to feel hot. Line a fine-mesh sieve with muslin (cheesecloth) and place it over a bowl. Pour in the parsley oil and set aside to strain overnight in the refrigerator.

Place the bowl into the freezer for 1½ hours, until the parsley water is frozen. (The mixture will separate and the water will freeze before the oil.) Pour out the oil and set aside.

In a robot coupe (or food processor), combine the garlic, egg yolks and vinegar and blend until smooth. Slowly incorporate the cold parsley oil and mix until emulsified. Season with salt and lemon juice.

Filling Heat the oil in a medium pan over medium heat. Add the onions and sauté for 7 minutes, until the onions are softened and translucent. Add the garlic and cook for another minute, until fragrant.

⤵

Assembly

1.5 L (50 fl oz/6¼ cups) vegetable
    stock
Aleppo chilli flakes, for sprinkling
Good-quality extra-virgin olive oil,
    for drizzling
Chervil, parsley and fennel fronds,
    for garnish

Add the rice and 850 ml (28½ fl oz/3½ cups) of water, then bring to a boil. Reduce the heat to medium-low, cover and simmer for 15–20 minutes, until nearly cooked. Fold in the fermented Kapya pepper, then set aside to cool.

Bring a large pan of salted water to a boil. Fill a large bowl with iced water.

Score the bottom of the cabbage to prevent damage to the leaves, then pull the leaves off. Add the cabbage to the boiling water and cook for 2 minutes. Transfer leaves, one by one, into the ice bath. Remove the cabbage stems.

Assembly Preheat the oven to 180°C/350°F (Gas mark 4).

Place 2 tablespoons of filling at the bottom of the leaf. Roll the leaf, tucking in the sides as you go along. Place the leaf into a baking dish. Repeat with the remaining leaves. Pour over the hot stock and cover with aluminium foil. Bake for 20 minutes, until the rice is cooked through.

To serve, spread a base of the emulsion onto a plate. Add the sarma, then finish with Aleppo chilli flakes and olive oil. Top with chervil, parsley and fennel fronds.

Leek and Onion Börek with Nettle and Smoked Cream

Serves 4

For the filling

2 tablespoons sunflower oil,
   for frying
6 leeks, white and light green parts
   only, thinly sliced
1 white onion, thinly sliced
6 cloves garlic, thinly sliced
Fine salt

For the smoked cream

300 ml (10 fl oz/1¼ cups) double
   (heavy) cream
1 large white-hot charcoal
100 g/3½ oz butter, room
   temperature

For the nettles

400 g/14 oz nettles
3½ tablespoons olive oil
1 onion, thinly sliced
6 cloves garlic, thinly sliced
100 ml (3½ fl oz/scant ½ cup)
   white wine
50 g (1¾ oz/1⅔ cups) spinach leaves

Assembly

1 package filo pastry, cut
   to the tray's dimensions
Melted butter, for brushing
1 egg, beaten

Filling Heat the oil in a large frying pan over high heat. Add the leeks, onions and garlic and sauté for 4 minutes, until translucent. Season with salt. The leeks should be vibrant and green still. Transfer to a baking sheet and set aside to cool. Place in the refrigerator until needed.

Smoked cream Place the cream in a cast-iron pot with a lid. Using tongs, very carefully lower the smouldering charcoal into the cream. It will eventually fizzle out. Set aside for an hour to infuse. Strain through a fine-mesh sieve. Whisk through cubes of butter.

Nettles Bring a pan of water to a boil. Fill a large bowl with iced water. Add the nettles and blanch for 10 seconds. Using a slotted spoon, transfer the nettles into the ice bath.

Heat the oil in a frying pan over medium heat. Add the onions and garlic and sauté for 3 minutes, until the onions are softened and translucent. Deglaze with the white wine, then add the nettles and sauté for 5 minutes.

Transfer the mixture to a blender and add the spinach. Blend until smooth, then strain through a fine-mesh sieve. Stir the mixture into the smoked cream.

Assembly Preheat the oven to 170°C/340°F (Gas mark 3). Line a baking sheet with parchment paper.

Lightly brush 10 sheets of filo with melted butter, then stack them. Spread the filling on top in an even layer. Lightly brush another 10 sheets of filo with melted butter and stack them over the filling.

Brush liberally with the beaten egg. Bake for 30 minutes, until golden. To serve, cut into 3 x 6-cm/1 ¼ x 2 ½-inch portions.

Börek with Fermented Parsley and Courgette

Serves 4

1 teaspoon olive oil
3 tablespoons finely chopped onions
2 cloves garlic, minced
Pinch of fine salt, plus extra to taste
300 g/10½ oz Turkish feta
  (*beyaz peynir*), crumbled
30 g/1 oz fermented parsley stems
  (page 158)
4 tablespoons finely chopped
  parsley
1 teaspoon dried purple basil
  (*reyhan*)
Lemon juice, to taste
1 package filo pastry
3½ tablespoons melted butter
1 egg, beaten

Assembly
3–4 yellow courgettes (zucchini),
  thinly sliced with a mandolin
2 teaspoons fine salt
4 teaspoons Smoked Olive Oil
  (page 100)
1 teaspoon lemon juice

Preheat the oven to 170°C/340°F (Gas mark 3).

Heat the oil in a small frying pan over medium heat. Add the onions, garlic and a pinch of salt and sauté for 5 minutes, until the onions are translucent.

In a large bowl, combine the onion-garlic mixture, the cheese, both parsleys and the purple basil. Season with salt and/or lemon juice.

Lay a sheet of filo onto the prepared baking sheet. Brush the top with the melted butter. Place another sheet on top, then brush with more melted butter. Add enough mixture to spread out into a thin layer, leaving a 1-cm/½-inch gap along the edges. Roll the filo, lengthwise, to create a log. Shape into a coil.

In a small bowl, combine the beaten egg and the remaining melted butter. Brush the egg wash over the pastry. Bake for 25 minutes.

Assembly Meanwhile, in a large bowl, combine all the ingredients. Mix well and set aside for 20 minutes.

Drape the courgette ribbons over the pastry to cover completely. Serve hot.

Aged Pollack with Carrot Fritters and Tarator

Serves 4

For the aged pollack
4 (100-g/3½-oz) pollack fillets
12 vine leaves, stems removed

For the tarator
2 heads fennel, thinly sliced
   on a mandolin
⅛ large white onion, thinly sliced
   on a mandolin
2 cloves garlic, thinly sliced on
   a mandolin, plus 1 small clove
   garlic, minced
½ teaspoon salt, plus extra to taste
250 ml (8 fl oz/1 cup) white wine
200 ml (7 fl oz/scant 1 cup)
   buttermilk
100 g (3½ oz/scant ½ cup) yogurt
3–4 tablespoons chopped dill

For the carrot fritters
2 potatoes, coarsely grated
1 carrot, coarsely grated
4½ tablespoons salt
2 tablespoons butter
¼ teaspoon Aleppo chilli flakes
¼ teaspoon ground cumin
¼ teaspoon black pepper
⅛ teaspoon smoked paprika
Vegetable oil, for deep-frying
Fennel fronds, for garnish

Aged pollack Wrap the pollack fillets in the vine leaves. Dry out in the refrigerator for 24 hours.

Tarator Heat the oil in a large frying pan over high heat. Add the fennel, onions and sliced garlic. Season with ½ teaspoon of salt to release the liquid, then add the white wine. Cover with a lid and cook for 45 minutes.

Uncover and simmer for 10 minutes, until the liquid has thickened and reduced by half. Transfer to a blender and purée until smooth. Strain through a fine-mesh sieve.

In a blender, combine 300 g/10½ fl oz of the fennel purée, the buttermilk, yogurt, minced garlic, dill and salt. Blend until smooth. Keep warm.

Carrot fritters Preheat the oven to 180°C/350°F (Gas mark 4).

In a large bowl, combine the potatoes, carrots and 4 tablespoons of salt. Set aside for 10 minutes. Squeeze out the liquid. Set aside.

Melt the butter in a small pan over medium heat. Add the remaining ½ tablespoon of salt and spices and heat for a minute, until fragrant. Fold the spiced butter through the carrots and potatoes.

Line a casserole (Dutch oven) with parchment paper. Pour in the mixture, then place another sheet of parchment on top. Cover with a lid and bake for 1 hour. Remove the pan from the oven, then place a 5-kg/11-lb weight evenly on top. Let the weight press in the refrigerator overnight.

Heat the oil in a deep fryer or a deep pan to 160°C/325°F. Portion the fritters into 2 x 4-cm/¾ x 1½-inch blocks. Working in batches to avoid overcrowding, carefully lower the fritters into the hot oil and deep-fry for 1½ minutes on each side, until golden. Transfer to a paper towel–lined plate and repeat with the remaining fritters.

Assembly Preheat a charcoal grill over high heat until the coals are white hot. Add the wrapped fillet and grill for a minute on each side, until the fish begins to firm up.

To serve, slice the pollack in half and arrange it on a plate. Add the fritters, then spoon the sauce to the side. Garnish with fennel fronds. Serve hot.

Apricot Sorbet

Serves 6

500 g/1 lb 2 oz apricots,
   stoned (pitted)
100 g (3½ oz/½ cup) sugar
50 g/1¾ oz glucose
Berries, cream or extra-virgin olive
   oil, to serve

Blend the apricots in a blender until smooth. Pour a quarter of the purée into a large pan. Add the sugar, glucose and 3 tablespoons of water and dissolve the mixture over medium heat. Fold in the remaining apricot purée and refrigerate for 1 hour to retain its fresh apricot flavour.

Pour the mixture into an ice-cream machine and churn, following the manufacturer's directions. Transfer into an ice-cream container and freeze for 1 hour until set.

Serve with berries, cream or oil.

Mountain Tea Rice Pudding with Sea Buckthorn and Honeycomb

Serves 6

For the rice pudding
200 ml (7 fl oz/scant 1 cup) milk
200 ml (7 fl oz/scant 1 cup) double
    (heavy) cream
200 g (7 oz/1 cup) sugar
20 g/¾ oz mountain tea (sideritis)
75 g (2½ oz/½ cup) pudding rice

For the sea buckthorn juice
100 g/3½ oz sea buckthorn
100 g/3½ oz glucose
4 tablespoons sugar

For the honeycomb
Non-stick cooking spray
3½ tablespoons sugar
2 tablespoons honey
1 tablespoon glucose
¾ teaspoon bicarbonate of soda
    (baking soda)
300 ml (10 fl oz/1¼ cups)
    double cream

To serve
Brown sugar, for sprinkling

Rice pudding In a small pan, combine all the ingredients except the pudding rice. Add 200 ml (7 fl oz/scant 1 cup) of water, then bring to a boil. Reduce the heat to medium-low and simmer for 15 minutes. Set aside to cool to room temperature, then refrigerate overnight to infuse.

Strain the mixture through a fine-mesh sieve into a pan, extracting as much milk as possible from the mountain tea. Add the pudding rice and soak for 30 minutes.

Bring the mixture to a boil, then reduce the heat to medium-low. Cover and simmer for 15–20 minutes, stirring occasionally, until the rice is cooked yet still retains a bite. Pour the mixture into a pan and refrigerate. This will set the shape for plating.

Sea buckthorn juice In a medium pan, combine all the ingredients and 200 ml (7 fl oz/scant 1 cup) of water. Cook over medium heat for 10 minutes, until the mixture has thickened. Transfer the mixture into a blender and pulse. (We don't want to break the seeds up too much.) Strain through a fine-mesh sieve and refrigerate until needed.

Honeycomb Spray a baking sheet with non-stick spray.

In a small pan, combine the sugar, honey and glucose. Melt over medium heat, then increase the heat to high and cook for another 2–3 minutes, until dark orange. Turn off the heat, add the bicarbonate of soda (baking soda) and stir until the mixture bubbles and froths.

Transfer the mixture into the prepared baking sheet. Set aside for 2 hours to set. Break up the honeycomb.

Heat the cream in a pan over medium-high heat, until it reaches 60°C/140°F. Add the honeycomb, one piece at a time, until completely melted.

To serve Warm up the rice pudding up in a pan. Set a ring mould in a bowl and spoon in the rice pudding. Liberally sprinkle over brown sugar, then remove the mould. Brûlée the sugar.

Pour in the sea buckthorn juice and honeycomb cream around the rice pudding. Serve warm.

Baklava

Serves 6

For the fig leaf syrup
Peel of 1 lemon
100 g (3½ oz/½ cup) caster
    (superfine) sugar
1½ tablespoons glucose
1½ tablespoons honey
1 teaspoon citric acid
5 fig leaves

For the blackberry cream
200 g (7 oz/1¾ cups) blackberries
100 ml (3½ fl oz/scant ½ cup)
    double (heavy) cream
4 tablespoons caster
    (superfine) sugar
2 tablespoons milk

For the baklava
2 (480-g/1 lb 1-oz) packs filo
    pastry sheets
500 g (1 lb 2 oz/4½ sticks)
    butter, melted
400 g (14 oz/3⅔ cups)
    chopped pecans
1½ teaspoons sea salt
150 g (5½ oz/scant ½ cup) honey
Cultured Kaymak (page 102),
    to serve (optional)
Fresh berries, to serve (optional)

Fig leaf syrup Combine all the ingredients except the fig leaves in a pan. Pour in 100 ml (3½ fl oz/scant ½ cup) of water and heat over medium heat until the mixture is translucent.

Place the fig leaves in a bowl, then add the hot syrup. Refrigerate overnight to infuse.

Strain the syrup through a fine-mesh sieve, squeezing out all the remaining liquid from the leaves. The macerated fig leaves can be used as a garnish and the syrup can be added to the kaymak when finishing the baklava.

Set aside to cool, then chill until needed.

Blackberry cream Combine all the ingredients in a blender and blend until smooth. Strain.

Baklava Preheat the oven to 170°C/340°F (Gas mark 3).

Stack one package of filo pastry sheets on a chopping (cutting) board. Trim the filo to the dimensions of the baking sheet. ❶ Place a filo sheet onto the baking sheet, then brush with melted butter. ❷❸ Ensure all areas are covered. Repeat until all the sheets are used up, finishing with a final layer of butter. ❹

In a bowl, combine the pecans and salt. ❺ Sprinkle the pecan mixture over the pastry. ❻ Spoon the honey on top. ❼ Layer the second package of filo pastry, lightly brushing butter over each sheet. ❽ Set in the refrigerator for at least 2 hours and up to 48 hours.

Bake for 30 minutes. Reduce the heat to 130°C/260°F (Gas mark ½) and bake for another 40 minutes. Increase the heat to 230°C/450°F (Gas mark 8) and bake for 10 minutes, until golden.

Pour the cold fig leaf syrup over the hot baklava, which will sizzle. ❾ Set aside to rest for 30 minutes, allowing the syrup to soak through. Serve with blackberry cream.

Serve hot or cold with cultured kaymak and berries, if desired.

Tahini Tart with Apple Butterscotch and Cherry Mahlep

During one of the lockdowns, I asked a few friends for guidance in tart pastry-making, specifically shortcrust pastry (basic pie dough). One of them said jokingly, 'Stop clowning around; stick to kebabs.' So I made a spite tart. And I wanted it to be great.

The flavour base is tahini – the main component of many breakfast tables and desserts – that has been infused into a butterscotch. The first attempt was heavy, so I added a sharp apple juice reduction with ample acidity to cut through the sweet roasted sesame flavour.

The diplomat cream (*crème diplomat*) base is enhanced with mahlep, a fragrant spice from roasted cherry seed kernels with an almond-like flavour. Its texture helps to aerate the density of the tart. It's the one dish I'm not allowed to remove from the menu. (I tried once to take it off, and a customer berated us as they had booked weeks in advance just to try it.)

You can purchase mahlep at Middle Eastern food stores.

Makes 16 slices

For the tart base
400 g (14 oz/2½ cups) plain
   (all-purpose) flour, plus extra
   for dusting
90 g (3¼ oz/¾ cup) icing
   (confectioners') sugar
4 tablespoons cornflour (cornstarch)
200 g (7 oz/1¾ sticks)
   chilled butter, cubed
2 eggs, beaten

Tart base In a food processor, combine all the ingredients except the eggs. Pulse until all the butter has broken down and it has a coarse breadcrumb-like texture. Pulse in one beaten egg and 1–2 teaspoons of iced water. Mix until it roughly comes together. ❶

Using your hands, pack the dough tightly together. ❷ Place on a sheet of clingfilm (plastic wrap), then pack it again and wrap up. Pat into a disk, then chill for 1 hour. Makes about 580 g/1 lb 5 oz.

Preheat the oven to 170ºC/340ºF (Gas mark 3).

Divide the dough in half. Generously dust a large sheet of parchment paper with flour. Add the dough, then dust it and a rolling pin with more the flour. Roll out the dough to a 1.5-mm/ ¹⁄₁₆-inch thickness. Wrap the dough around the rolling pin, then lay the dough into a 28-cm/11-inch loose-bottomed tart pan.

↴

For the butterscotch

200 ml (7 fl oz/scant 1 cup)
   apple juice
670 g/1 lb 8 oz butter
540 g (1 lb 5 oz/2⅔ cups) dark
   brown sugar
540 ml (18 fl oz/2½ cups) double
   (heavy) cream
340 ml (12 oz/1½ cups) tahini
2 tablespoons sea salt

For the crème pâtissière

120 g (4 oz/generous ½ cup) sugar
6 egg yolks
2 tablespoons plain (all-purpose) flour
2½ tablespoons cornflour
75 g (2¾ oz/¾ cup) mahlep
550 ml (18 fl oz/2½ cups) milk
600 ml (20 fl oz/2½ cups)
   double cream

Carefully push out the dough evenly into the corners and ridges of the tin. Avoid having thinner parts, which will crack in the oven. Trim the edges and use the excess dough to fill any gaps. Square off the edges for a tidy and even finish. Using a fork, prick around the edges and the centre of the tart. Line the tart with clingfilm and fill with pie weights (baking beans), ensuring it covers the entire base for the blind-baking. (I mix flour and dried chickpeas in a freezer bag, which helps to distribute the weight evenly.) Blind-bake for 20 minutes. Remove the weights.

Fill any large cracks with left-over pastry. Brush the interior with the remaining beaten egg and bake for another 13 minutes.

Butterscotch Pour the apple juice into a small saucepan. Simmer until the mixture is reduced to 4 tablespoons.

Melt the butter in a large pan over medium heat. ❸❹ Stir in the dark brown sugar and apple juice reduction, then reduce the heat to medium-low. ❺ Cook for 10 minutes, until homogenised and thickened. Remove the pan from the heat.

Stir in the double (heavy) cream, tahini and salt. ❻ Reduce the heat to very low and cook for another 5 minutes, until everything is incorporated. Stir frequently to prevent it from burning and from splitting. Hold it at a temperature of 45°C/113°F, then carefully pour the mixture into the tart base. ❼ Chill in the fridge overnight to set.

Crème pâtissière In a bowl, combine the sugar and egg yolks and mix until pale and creamy. ❽ Sift in the flour, cornflour (cornstarch) and mahlep and whisk until well mixed.

Bring the milk to a boil in a separate pan. Gradually ladle it into the egg mixture, whisking continuously. ❾ Return to the pan and cook over medium-low heat for 15–20 minutes, stirring frequently with a spatula, to prevent the bottom from catching. The mixture is ready when it becomes too thick to mix with ease. Strain the crème patisserie through a fine-mesh sieve into a bowl. Set aside to cool, then cover with clingfilm and press down gently to ensure contact with the surface of the crème patisserie. Refrigerate for 1 hour.

Whip the cream in a bowl until stiff peaks form. Fold in an equal amount of crème patisserie. Transfer the mixture to a piping (pastry) bag and pipe onto the tart.

And in the End, Everyone Leaves

The customer's experience is fleeting, intense, mesmeric. Upon entry, smoke and fire infuse their nostrils and saliva floods their glands. They eat, drink, interact and leave. Most return, but it is always an exchange. Money for food and service. Money for an experience. That is the nature of the job. You try to remain detached. Customers come, but customers go and return to their lives. It is the contract of our agreement, like every other eatery. They are the lifeblood of the business and loyal champions of Mangal II, but we cannot provide them sustenance all the time. They eat here when they feel like it, and we are at their mercy. The customer is God. And God leaves.

Suppliers are passionate. They fish, tend to land, ship over plates, forage mushrooms and collect your dirty aprons and fix your boiler and delicately pick your micro-herbs. Sometimes, they will try and fuck you over, but most of the time they are reliable, well-intentioned and come to your rescue. We need them and they need us, and it's one big intricate web to maintain the ecosystem. You fall out with some suppliers, and you begrudgingly cut ties with others. Some go bust; other prospects approach you daily. It's a hundred on-the-go relationships at once. It's speed dating. It's addictive and exhausting. It's transactional, always transactional. And in the end, the supplier does their job and leaves. Sometimes for good.

The competition has been cutthroat. Back in the day, there were three fellow ocakbaşı restaurants on our road offering a similar menu at a slightly lower price. By the mid-2000s, this had expanded four-fold. I suspect many from the Turkish community saw the success of Mangal I & II and thought they could do the same but better. They tried to earn more by charging less and offering more freebies. As a basic example, I created a £10 lunch menu a decade ago: one starter, one main, one soft drink. It was the first ocakbaşı of its kind to do so in the area. It didn't do well or propel us yet, one week later, a neighbouring restaurant offered the exact same menu for £9. We felt the effects of local competition every day, all the time. Our survival was constantly under threat. Struggling to stand out on a road where other restaurants were eerily like ours, Google and Tripadvisor reviews became so impactful as customers had to distinguish us from a stretch of land where all food and prices were evenly matched. We were at the mercy of our clientele. When BYOB was introduced by competitors at no extra charge, it ruined a huge source of our income as we felt forced to apply the same policy due to the risk of losing customers. We were all pissing against the wind in a saturated market. Things felt bleak.

Thank God, Sertaç went to Copenhagen and returned triumphant; otherwise, we might not be here today. Bar Mangal I and Cırrık, nearly all the other restaurants have either shut down or changed hands. They've all left. They all leave.

The hype, the publicity and the fame come in waves. According to my father, customers and media features, our restaurant was innovative and greatly acclaimed when it first opened. It had an expansive, rich and unmatched mezze offering, a vast array of kebabs and the lucrative house-made *yaprak döner*. Waiters wore smart shirts and ties; tablecloths were ironed and impeccable. Prices were ludicrously low and the cooking standard admirably high. Awards and recognition were in abundance: *Time Out, The Independent,* etc. Over the next decade, restaurants, particularly Turkish ocakbaşı, became plentiful and our star dimmed a little. It continued this way for a long time.

Then, I started the whole Twitter nonsense, and we were again very much in the public lexicon. A Turkish restaurant tweeting witty, irreverent social commentary? What?! The tweets kept going viral, and the hype-train choo-choo-chose us as its next destination. Strangers latched on. Jobs offers flooded in. Media agencies wanted a piece of me, but inevitably, as I was simultaneously running Mangal II, I was fired from each role.

Eventually, my tweets were less sacrilegious, and the angsty output subsided. I had more to focus on: work, my young family, myself. Things died down and the hype-train departed. I was left with a struggling restaurant while my dad enjoyed semi-retirement and my brother developed as a chef in Copenhagen. It felt like everyone left, including, slowly by slowly, old regulars, as I struggled to keep the business afloat.

With the volatility of success and popularity, and its subsequent challenges, things took a new course in 2020 with Sertaç's return and our joint direction; the accolades and plaudits returned. It was overwhelming at times. Years of silence and unfavourable comparisons to Mangal I were replaced with this sudden outburst of love as we embraced a new voice. It was bittersweet but, as time passed, I realised that it's just what London was missing: a restaurant with Turkish tones and structure that were modernised, good quality and refined in a relaxed setting with natural wines. We had young, chic staff and a strong family backstory. A legacy.

It comes in waves, as it always has with Mangal II. Soon enough, we'll be less talked about and out of the spotlight. There's always that risk, but the integrity and honesty remain.

Staff members leave without fail. Some move onto new and more prestigious pastures, using the restaurant as a stepping stone for their CVs (particularly chefs) without fully learning much here because they're always after the next thing to swing their dick around. Others simply quit the industry because it's not their day passion. Some find a better-paying role. Some you fall out with. Some become enemies. Some continue to be your closest friends long after their departure. And some, sadly, you let go – though this is always a last resort. Some you do backflips for to prevent them from leaving, knowing their heart's not in it long term. It's a painful game of cat and mouse with one clear conclusion: they'll leave. Everyone leaves. The restaurant remains. Don't get too attached, and always be prepared for that fatal blow. Everyone leaves.

In the end, everyone leaves. Everything ends. Those involved with the restaurant's life, the produce, the experiences, the debt and the earnings. Perhaps, perhaps even Mangal II. We won't be around forever.

What will remain is a legacy in this book – a tangible embodiment of our family's work and passion. Our story. Ali and Sertaç Dirik's recipes. Our name on your shelves. It took 30 years to get here, to pave our journey and to publish that expression in a book. We are grateful for the opportunity to share our family story. And if you can take away anything from this (beyond the delicious dishes you can replicate at home), it's that we care and take pride in what we do. It always felt honest to us. From the fields of inner Anatolia to the streets of London, from the flame of the ocakbaşı to your table. Thank you.

— Ferhat

Leaving

Mangal II is now a very different restaurant from what it was thirty years ago. Years of testing, tweaking, starting over, repeat. Finally, we've reached a moment of clarity. The restaurant is busy every night, and we have regulars again... with foodies amongst them. People travel from the opposite end of the city to try our food, and with it comes a respect and admiration for Turkish cuisine – this is important, considering our restaurant's history.

The restaurant is in a healthy state, and massive debt is a stress of the past. Both front of house and back of house comprise the most incredible, intelligent, hard-working and dedicated people I've had the pleasure of working with.

It's healed the bond with my family. As some may know, when you grow up in a family business, the state of your relationships is connected directly to the health of the business. The lessons Ferhat and I have learned, the extremities we've reached and the greatest obstacles we've overcome together are nothing short of a miracle. We set up a restaurant that was in debt the day it opened without any help from investors, banks or our family. We adapted and bent in every direction but never broke. I'm so unbelievably proud of our achievement, together.

I have reconnected with my roots. As a British-born Turk who grew up in a Turkish restaurant, I never dove deeply into my culture – the wish is to feel more English, attract less attention and blend in. Within the last few years, I found my place in the world, beyond the development of a restaurant. My questions of identity, belonging and my people have become clearer. While I feel more connected to Turkey, I am left in a grey area having grown up in England. I'm either too English for the Turks and too Turkish for the English, which is OK. I'm a Londoner. I love my city. It gave me the space to develop my ideas of Turkish cuisine, using products from passionate British purveyors, and create something wholly different. Oftentimes, it can be frustrating, but it's my home and where this story is set.

It's difficult to describe my relationship with Mangal II as I've experienced every emotion in that building. It went from being my teenage prison to a ladder with an endless reach. I'd dedicated three years to a cause with very specific guidelines and familial pressure; it was not allowed to fail. The restaurant supports my mum, dad, my brother and, in turn, my niece and nephew.

Trial and error become the guiding light, and the need to push myself and make discoveries is the catalyst that keeps the restaurant busy. Mangal II has become a beloved spot. To change it for the sake of change, at this point, would defy the reason why we started this process in the first place. It was a failing restaurant, and now it works.

I have spent most of my life in this space, and now that all is settled, it's time for me to figure out what my own cooking looks like. I am forever grateful for the opportunity bestowed upon me as it's impacted my life positively in so many ways. Ferhat and the team will continue to steer Mangal II from strength to strength, and I'm excited to watch it develop and give more meaning to the name. I'll still be involved from the sidelines – it's important to pass the torch and watch it develop organically in its current form. It's not typical for a restaurant to turn thirty; the building could have folded multiple times over the years. In truth, it feels like it was holding out for its renaissance, and now its identity is stronger than ever.

It was never up to us when Mangal II ended – it's a living entity and it's clearly not going anywhere, anytime soon. It will let us know when it's ready. Thirty more years? Let's see.

— Sertaç

In Conversation with Ali: Part II

Ferhat: Was it important for this restaurant to keep going in the long term?
Ali: I am in favour of establishments that have been passed on for at least three generations, from grandfather to child to grandchild. Long-lasting restaurants, they have a spiritual wealth and value. They provide communities with trust and security. Equally, I am also very against hard-formed places that have become easily spent. Let it always run; let it always serve; allow the public to always return to it as a second home with comfort and acceptance. A restaurant is a family's insurance, and it should always live on.

F: Do you have any predictions for the future, for Sertaç or me?
A: Even if my children study and work in different industries, they should continue to run the restaurant to provide a stable income for themselves and raise their own children with the same expectations. They should all have a good quality of life but also honour what has been passed down from father to son. I wish for this.

F: How do you feel about Sertaç stepping away from the day-to-day running of the kitchen and embarking on a new path?
A: First of all, I don't accept the notion that Sertaç has left Mangal II. Today's young and dynamic chefs all manage multiple restaurants at once. It's a matter of having a strong team. He won't do it alone. He will form a team and train them. If there is trust and delegation, I believe he can succeed and run more than one restaurant. Also, in the long run, I'm against one restaurant having two partners because it won't allow room for growth and success. The most important thing is to take risks, and Sertaç is doing the right thing – remaining stagnant will eventually drains one's energy and saps their potential future success.

F: Presumably, this applies more for chefs?
A: Yes, certainly for chefs. Today, in London or any other major city in the world, there are many successful people who own multiple restaurants. These are all achieved with a good team. It's never one person doing it all, but often a strong individual who sits at the top and trains others and delegates accordingly, with a tight network. This is the formula to growth.

F: Do you have any further thoughts?
A: I wish the continued success for all of my children. And I'm sure they will continue to succeed. May God grant them good health. I always want to see them do well, to do even better and further themselves. And I want to thank you all for allowing me an early [retirement]. I love you all dearly.

Index

Acknowledgements

Ferhat

Thank you to Zeki and Juno, my children, for inspiring me to produce something they'll hopefully someday look back on with pride.

I'd like to thank the team, including Phaidon's Emilia Terragni for her support of our original idea and Michelle Meade for her guidance and patience and 'getting' my voice; Studio Cantina, the best designers out there and all-round good eggs; and my good pal Justin de Souza for being a photographer extraordinaire. To all Mangal II suppliers, staff and customers – past and present – my essays wouldn't exist without you.

I'd also like to thank my childhood friend Zoheir Ebrahim for his constant encouragement and critical input. To my brother, working together has been an experience of heaven and hell and all in between but, ultimately, I wouldn't change a thing. My sister and my mum for being my rock, and my dad for his life's output. And finally, to my cousin Mehmet Dirik, who sadly passed twelve years ago and worked many years at Mangal II. Thank you for always treating the younger, teenage version of me with kindness, compassion and love.

Sertaç

I am indebted to my friends and family. Thank you to Jules St-Cyr, Nik Harmsen, A-hyeon Lee and Alan McQueen for giving me solace, knowledge and true friendship; to Orlando Ribeiro, my first real mentor; to Elliot Bernardo for the art of learning how to learn; and to Matt Orlando for proving that love is a greater tool than fear. I'd like to extend my gratitude to every single incredible individual who helped shape Mangal II.

Thank you to my mum, Cemile, for showing me the beauty of the cooking and giving us all the care in the world and to my sister, Ayşegül, who sparked my love of art and colour, the catalyst of my creative thinking. To my dad, Ali, for gifting me with his trade and for being my port of call for knowledge. Lastly, to my brother, Ferhat. The reason behind my love for restaurants. He took the world on his shoulders so I could develop independently. He is the reason why Mangal II stands today.

About the Authors

Ferhat

Ferhat Dirik, the managing director of Mangal II, took reins of the family business in 2015 and, with his brother, Sertaç, reinvented the restaurant to critical acclaim. His irreverent Twitter account, widely regarded as one of the most original voices on social media, amassed 80,000 followers. His vision, combined with Sertaç's talent, has led the restaurant's success.

Sertaç

At twenty-three, Sertaç Dirik worked at some of Copenhagen's finest restaurants, including Noma's sister restaurant 108 and Matt Orlando's zero-waste Amass. During the pandemic, he returned home to helm his family's iconic East London restaurant, Mangal II, with his brother, Ferhat. Within two years, Sertaç was hailed as one of the UK's most exciting rising stars, having been recognised as 'Young Chef of the Year 2022' (*Observer Food Monthly*) and 'London's Brightest' (*Time Out*, 2022).

Phaidon Press Limited
2 Cooperage Yard
London E15 2QR

Phaidon Press Inc.
111 Broadway
New York, NY 10006

phaidon.com

First published 2024
© 2024 Phaidon Press Limited

ISBN 978 1 83866 849 5

Commissioning Editor:
Emilia Terragni

Project Editor:
Michelle Meade

Production Controller:
Zuzana Cimalova

Design:
Ana Teodoro, Cantina

Photography: Justin De Souza
Images on pages 15, 18 and 19 courtesy of the authors
Images on pages 142 and 145 courtesy of Matt Austin

Printed in China

Publisher's Acknowledgements
Phaidon would like to thank James Brown, Ali Dirik, Marnie Lamb,
João Mota and Ellie Smith.

Recipe Notes

Unless otherwise specified:
Butter is always unsalted.
All sugar is granulated.
All herbs are fresh.
All cream is 36–40% fat heavy whipping cream.
All milk is whole at 3% fat, homogenised and
lightly pasteurized.
All salt is fine sea salt.

Cooking times are for guidance only, as individual
ovens vary. If using a fan (convection) oven, follow
the manufacturer's directions concerning oven
temperatures. Exercise a high level of caution when
following recipes involving any potentially hazardous
activity, including the use of high temperatures,
open flames, slaked lime, and when deep-frying.
In particular, when deep-frying, add food carefully to
avoid splashing, wear long sleeves, and never leave
the pan unattended.

Some recipes include raw or very lightly cooked
eggs, meat or fish, and fermented products. These
should be avoided by the elderly, infants, pregnant
people, convalescents and anyone with an impaired
immune system.

Exercise caution when making fermented products,
ensuring all equipment is spotlessly clean, and seek
expert advice if in any doubt.

When no quantity is specified, for example of oils,
salts and herbs used for finishing dishes or for deep-
frying, quantities are discretionary and flexible.

All herbs, shoots, flowers and leaves should be
picked fresh from a clean source.

Exercise caution when foraging for ingredients;
any foraged ingredients should be eaten only if
an expert has deemed them safe to eat.

Measurement Notes

All spoon and cup measurements are level unless
otherwise stated.

Australian standard tablespoons are 20 ml,
so Australian readers are advised to use
3 teaspoons in place of 1 tablespoon when
measuring small quantities.